Passing the

Numeracy Skills Test

7th Edition

Mark Patmore

Los Angeles I London I New Delhi
Singapore I Washington DC I Melbourne

Learning Matters
An imprint of SAGE Publications Ltd
1 Oliver's Yard
55 City Road
London EC1Y 1SP

SAGE Publications Inc.
2455 Teller Road
Thousand Oaks, California 91320

SAGE Publications India Pvt Ltd
B 1/I 1 Mohan Cooperative Industrial Area
Mathura Road
New Delhi 110 044

SAGE Publications Asia-Pacific Pte Ltd
3 Church Street
#10-04 Samsung Hub
Singapore 049483

Editor: Amy Thornton
Production controller: Chris Marke
Project management: Deer Park Productions,
Tavistock, Devon
Marketing manager: Lorna Patkai
Cover design: Wendy Scott
Typeset by: C&M Digitals (P) Ltd, Chennai, India
Printed and bound in Great Britain

First published in 2000 by Learning Matters Ltd.

Second edition published in 2001. Reprinted in 2001
(twice) and 2002 (twice). Third edition published
in 2003. Reprinted in 2004 (twice), 2005 (twice)
and 2006 (twice). Fourth edition published in 2008.
Reprinted in 2009 (twice). Fifth edition published in
2012. Reprinted in 2013. Revised fifth edition printed
in 2013. Reprinted in 2013. Sixth edition published in
2015. Seventh edition published in 2018.

Library of Congress Control Number: 2017954830

British Library Cataloguing in Publication data

A catalogue record for this book is available from
the British Library.

ISBN 978-1-5264-1922-4
ISBN 978-1-5264-1923-1 (pbk)

At SAGE we take sustainability seriously. Most of our products are printed in the UK using FSC papers and boards.
When we print overseas we ensure sustainable papers are used as measured by the PREPS grading system.
We undertake an annual audit to monitor our sustainability.

Passing the

Numeracy Skills Test

WITHDRAWN

Contents

Acknowledgements

The glossary is reproduced courtesy of the Standards and Testing Agency. Permission to reproduce such copyright material does not extend to any material which is identified as being the copyright of a third party or any photographs. Authorisation to reproduce such material would need to be obtained from the copyright holders.

About the author

Mark Patmore is a former senior lecturer in mathematical education at the School of Education at Nottingham Trent University and is currently working as an associate lecturer at the University of Derby. He has worked in teacher education with Bishop Grosseteste University and with training providers, and he also provided CPD for teachers of mathematics. After some years as a numeracy consultant for the Teacher Training Agency, Mark was for several years one of the writers for the numeracy skills tests and then became a member of the Test Review Group managed by Alpha*Plus* Consultancy which monitored the writing of the tests.

Mark was Chief Examiner for the Cambridge Award in Mathematics, and was chief examiner for functional skills in mathematics and has been involved with assessing and verifying a range of educational qualifications. He is the author or co-author of a number of publications for both GCSE and Key Stage 3 Mathematics.

Series introduction

The QTS skills tests

All applicants for initial teacher training (ITT) courses are required to have passed the qualified teacher status (QTS) skills tests in both numeracy and literacy before the start of their course.

This requirement applies to those intending to follow an employment-based route into teaching, such as the School Direct programme, as well as those intending to take the PGCE route. The requirement also applies to unqualified teachers seeking QTS by following the Assessment Only route.

Note: Applicants will need to take the proof of their application to ITT with them on the day(s) of their test(s).

The tests cover skills in:

- numeracy
- literacy

Applicants will be allowed three attempts to pass the numeracy skills test and three attempts to pass the literacy skills test. The first attempt is free but each of the two resits is currently charged at £19.25. Applicants who fail three attempts are 'barred' from making further attempts for a period of two years.

The tests will demonstrate that a teacher can apply skills in numeracy and literacy to the degree necessary for their use in the day-to-day work in a school. They do not assess the subject knowledge required for teaching. The tests are taken online by booking a time at a specified centre, they are marked instantly and the result, along with feedback on that result, will be given to the applicant before they leave the centre.

There is more information about the skills tests and the specified centres on the following website: http://www.education.gov.uk/sta/professional.

Titles in this series

This series of books is designed to help you become familiar with the skills you will need to pass the tests and to practise questions on each of the topic areas to be tested.

Passing the Numeracy Skills Test (seventh edition)
Mark Patmore
ISBN 978-1-5264-1922-4
ISBN 978-1-5264-1923-1 (pbk)

Passing the Literacy Skills Test (fifth edition)
Jim Johnson and Bruce Bond
ISBN 978-1-5264-4017-4
ISBN 978-1-5264-4018-1 (pbk)

Introduction

Introduction to the test

The numeracy skills test is a computerised test, which is divided into two sections:

- section 1 for the mental arithmetic questions;
- section 2 for the written questions known as 'on-screen' questions.

The **mental arithmetic** section is an audio test heard through headphones. Calculators are not allowed, but noting numbers and jotting down working will be permitted. (You should be issued with either a wipe-clean board and pen, or with paper to help with this.) There are 12 questions in this section. Note: this section must be answered first; each question has a fixed time in which you must answer (18 seconds); you cannot return to a question if you later wish to change your answer. Questions will be asked to test your ability to carry out mental calculations using fractions, percentages, measurement, conversions and time (see the detailed content list on page 5).

The **'on-screen'** questions: there are 16 written questions in this section. Seven questions are focused on *interpreting* and using written data and nine are focused on *solving* written arithmetic problems. Questions and answers will be in one of the following forms:

- multiple-choice questions where you will choose the single correct response from a fixed number of alternative answers;
- multiple-response questions where you choose single or multiple correct statements from a fixed number of given statements;
- questions that require a single answer;
- questions where you will select the answer by pointing and clicking on the correct point in a table, chart or graph (to change an answer click on an alternative point);
- questions where you will select your answer from a number of alternative answers and place the answer into the answer box provided (to change an answer drag it back to its original position and choose another).

In this part of the test you can use the 'on-screen' calculator. You answer questions using the mouse and the keyboard and you can move between questions by using the 'next' and 'previous' buttons. You can return to questions either by using the 'flag' button and then the 'review' button or by waiting until the end of the test when you will have the option of reviewing all the questions – provided there is time!

There are a total of (12 + 16 =) 28 questions. Each question is worth 1 mark. Think of the pass mark as being 18. You do not have to gain a certain number of marks in each section so you could gain 4 marks in the mental arithmetic section and 14 in the on-screen section or 7 marks in the mental section and 11 marks in the on-screen section or....

Time for the test

The time limit for the whole test is approximately 48 minutes. At the end of which the test will shut down automatically. (Note: The mental test will take about 12 minutes and the on-screen test will take about 36 minutes.)

The contexts for the questions

One of the aims of the numeracy skills test is to ensure that teachers have the skills and understanding necessary to analyse the sort of data that is now used in schools. Consequently most questions will be set within contexts such as:

- national test data;

- target setting and school improvement data;

- pupil progress and attainment over time;

- special educational needs (SEN);

- GCSE subject choices and results.

Hints and advice

The mental arithmetic, audio section

Each mental arithmetic question is heard twice. After the first reading an answer box appears on the screen. You will have a short time – 18 seconds – to work out the answer and type it into the answer box, after which the next question will automatically appear. As mentioned earlier, you cannot move forwards or backwards between questions. At the start of the test you will hear a practice question which you do not have to answer but do use it to check that the sound and volume are appropriate. If not, notify the supervisor in the test room.

- Concentrate the first time the question is read, and note down the key numbers. For example, a question could be 'In a class of 30 pupils, 24 are boys. What fraction are girls?' You should jot down 30 and 24. The second time the question is heard, concentrate on what to do with those numbers (for example, $30 - 24 = 6$ (so there are 6 girls) then $6/30 = 1/5$).

- Start to work out the answer as soon as you have the information. You may be able to do this while you hear the second reading of the question.

- If you cannot answer a question don't worry or panic – enter a likely answer, then forget it. Remember, you don't need to get every single question right.

- Note that you don't have to worry about units, i.e. £ or € or cm, for example. The units will appear in the answer box.

- Listen carefully to what the question requires in the answer. For example, a question could ask for a time 'using the 24-hour clock', or an answer 'to the nearest whole number', or 'to two decimal places'. (There are notes on this in Chapter 3.)

- Fractions need to be entered in the lowest terms. For example, 6/8 should be entered as 3/4 and 7/28 should be entered as 1/4.

- Practise using mental strategies. For example, purchasing five books that cost £5.99 can be worked out by multiplying 5 x £6 (£30) and subtracting 5 x 1p (5p) to give the answer of £29.95.

- Remember the link between fractions and percentages – see Chapter 1.

The on-screen questions

- Try not to spend more than two minutes on any one question and keep an eye on the time remaining. If you think you are exceeding the time then move on – you can always return to any you still need to complete at the end of the test and insert an answer. Try not to leave any answers blank at the end of the test.

- Read each question carefully. For example, a question may ask for the percentage of pupils who achieved grade 4 and above. Don't just look at those who gained grade 4; the question included the words 'and above', so you need to include those who achieved 'above', i.e. achieved grade 5, grade 6, and so on.

- Check that you are giving the correct information in the answer. A table may give you details of the number of marks a pupil achieved but the question may be asking for a percentage score.

The on-screen calculator

When the mental arithmetic section of the test is finished, a basic four-function calculator will be available on the screen for you to use for the rest of the test. No other calculators can be used. You can move the calculator around the screen using the mouse. The on-screen calculator works through the mouse and through the number pad on the keyboard. If you wish to use the number pad you must ensure that the number lock key 'Num Lock' is activated.

Notes on using the on-screen calculator

- To cancel an operation, press CE .

- Always use the 'clear' button C on the calculator before beginning a new calculation.

- Always check the display of the calculator to make sure that the number shown is what you wanted.

- Check calculations and make sure that your final answer makes sense in the context of the question. For example, the number of pupils gaining 60% in a test will not be greater than the size of the cohort or group.

Other hints

1. Rounding up and down

- Make sure that any instructions to round an answer up or down are followed – or the answer will be marked as incorrect.

- Use the context to make sure whether a decimal answer should be rounded up or down. For example, an answer of 16.4 lessons for a particular activity is clearly not appropriate and the answer would need to be rounded up to 17 lessons.

- Questions may specify that the answer should be rounded to the nearest whole number or be rounded to two decimal places. See the notes at the start of Chapter 3.

- When carrying out calculations relating to money, the answer shown on the calculator display will need to be rounded to the nearest penny (unless otherwise indicated). Hence, if calculating in pounds, round to two decimal places to show the number of pence. If 10.173 is the answer in pounds on the calculator display, rounding to the nearest penny gives £10.17. NB: Answers to money calculations should have no decimal places or 2 decimal places. Thus an answer should be given as £4.10 and not as £4.1, and £10 must be written as £10 or £10.00 and not £10.0.

2. Answering multi-stage questions

The calculator provided is not a scientific calculator and therefore care needs to be taken with 'mixed operations' (i.e. calculations using several function keys). It is important that the function keys are pressed in the appropriate order for the calculation. It may also be useful to note down answers to particular stages of the calculation.

It is important to remember to carry out the calculation required by the question in the following order: any calculation within brackets followed by division/multiplication followed by addition and/or subtraction. Thus, the answer to the calculation $2 + 3 \times 4$ is 14 and not 20; the answer to $\dfrac{18}{3+6}$ is $\dfrac{18}{9} = 2$; and the answer to $\dfrac{18}{3} + 6 = 6 + 6 = 12$. See the notes at the start of Chapter 3.

3. Dealing with fractions

Although fractions will appear in the usual format within a question (for example, $\frac{3}{4}$), to enter a fraction in an answer, use the 'forward slash' key (for example, 'one-half' would be entered as 1/2). Therefore using the on-screen calculator to calculate with fractions, it is probably easier to deal with the fraction first, converting it into a decimal, and then multiply by this decimal. For example, to calculate $\frac{5}{8}$ of 320, first find $5 \div 8 = 0.625$. Multiply 0.625 by 320, obtaining 200 as the answer.

How to use this book

The book is divided into six chapters.

Chapter 1: this very short chapter has been included to remind you of the basic arithmetic processes. The majority of you will be able to miss this unit out, but some may welcome a chance to revise fractions, decimals, percentages, etc.

Chapter 2: this chapter provides guidance, examples and questions for the mental arithmetic section. Look at the revision checklist on the next page for a list of the content areas that could be tested.

Chapter 3: this chapter provides guidance, examples and questions on solving written arithmetic problems. Look at the revision checklist on the next page and over onto page 6 for a list of the content areas that could be tested.

Chapter 4: this chapter provides guidance, examples and questions on interpreting and using written data. Look at the revision checklist on page 6 for a list of the content areas that could be tested.

Chapter 5: this includes a practice mental arithmetic test, and a full practice onscreen test for you to work through.

Chapter 6: this contains answers and key points for all the questions in the main chapters and for the sample tests.

In each chapter, the additional required knowledge, language and vocabulary are explained, and worked examples of the type of questions to be faced are provided together with the practice questions. The answers for these questions are given in Chapter 6, together with further advice and guidance on solutions.

Revision checklists

The following charts show in detail the coverage of the three main chapters and the practice tests. You can use the checklists in your revision to make sure that you have covered all the key content areas.

Revision checklist for Chapter 2: Mental arithmetic

Content	Question
2a Time – varied contexts	1, 7, 18, 20, 25, 34
2b Amounts of money varied contexts	12, 38, 42, 43, 44
2c Proportion – answer as a fraction	37
2d Proportion – answer as a percentage	27
2e Proportion – answer as a decimal	22
2f Fractions	16, 29, 45
2g Decimals	21, 32, 39
2h Percentages – varied contexts	2, 11, 19, 20, 24, 26, 28, 30, 35, 42
2i Measurements – distance	36
2j Measurements – area	23
2k Measurements – other	40
2l Conversions – from one currency to another	44
2m Conversions – from fractions to decimals	15
2n Conversions – from decimals to fractions	
2o Conversions – from percentages to fractions	31
2p Conversions – from fractions to percentages	4, 9, 13, 33
2q Conversions – other	6
2r Combination of one or more of addition, subtraction, multiplication, division (may involve amounts of money or whole numbers)	3, 5, 8, 10, 14, 17, 41

Revision checklist for Chapter 3: Solving written arithmetic problems

(Note: Only the main references are used; many questions will cover more than one reference.)

Content	Question
3a Time – varied contexts	7, 17, 29, 31, 33
3b Amounts of money	2, 11, 57, 60
3c Proportion – answer as a fraction	14
3d Proportion – answer as a percentage	14
3e Proportion – answer as a decimal	13, 14, 62

(Continued)

Content	Question
3f Ratios	3, 59, 60
3g Percentages – varied contexts	4, 5, 6, 8, 9, 12, 13, 18, 24, 27, 39, 41, 42, 47, 53, 56, 59, 62
3h Fractions	10, 19, 41, 54, 57
3i Decimals	
3j Measurements – distance	21, 26, 28, 30, 36
3k Measurements – area	22
3l Conversions – from one currency to another	2
3m Conversions – from fractions to decimals or vice versa	14
3n Conversions – other, including measures	15, 16, 20, 24, 38, 39, 48, 61
3o Averages – mean	11, 23, 45, 58
3p Averages – median	23
3q Averages – mode	
3r Range	11, 35, 56
3s Averages – combination	1, 34, 44
3t Using simple formulae	32, 40, 43, 46, 49, 50, 51, 52, 55

Revision checklist for Chapter 4: Interpreting and using written data

(Note: Only the main references are used; many questions will cover more than one reference.)

Content	Question
4a Identify trends over time	9, 13, 17, 19, 21
4b Make comparisons in order to draw conclusions	2, 5, 10, 11, 12, 14, 23, 24
4c Interpret and use information	1, 3, 4, 6, 7, 8, 15, 16, 18, 20
3o Averages	9

Revision checklist for the practice mental arithmetic test

Content	Question
1a Time – varied contexts	6, 11
1b Amounts of money – varied contexts	7
1c Proportion – answer as a fraction	
1d Proportion – answer as a percentage	
1e Proportion – answer as a decimal	
1f Fractions	1, 12
1g Decimals	
1h Percentages – varied contexts	2, 3, 5, 9, 10
1i Measurements – distance	
1j Measurements – area	
1k Measurements – other	

Content	Question
1l Conversions – from one currency to another	
1m Conversions – from fractions to decimals	
1n Conversions – from decimals to fractions	
1o conversions – from percentages to fractions	8
1p Conversions – from fractions to percentages	
1q Conversions – other	4
1r Combination of one or more of addition, subtraction, multiplication, division (may involve amounts of money or whole numbers)	1, 11

Revision checklist for the practice on-screen test

Content	Question
4a Identify trends over time	3, 9
4b Make comparisons in order to draw conclusions	1, 4, 8
4c Interpret and use information	2, 6, 7
3a Time – varied contexts	5
3b Amounts of money	10
3c Proportion – answer as a fraction	
3d Proportion – answer as a percentage	14
3e Proportion – answer as a decimal	
3f Ratios	
3g Percentages – varied contexts	4, 15, 16
3h Fractions	13
3i Decimals	
3j Measurements – distance	
3k Measurements – area	
3l Conversions – from one currency to another	
3m Conversions – from fractions to decimals or vice versa	
3n Conversions – other	
3o Averages – mean	
3p Averages – median	
3q Averages – mode	
3r Range	
3s Averages – combination	
3t Given formulae	9, 11

1 | Key knowledge

Fractions, decimals and percentages

Essentially fractions, decimals and percentages are the same things. They are all ways of writing numbers.

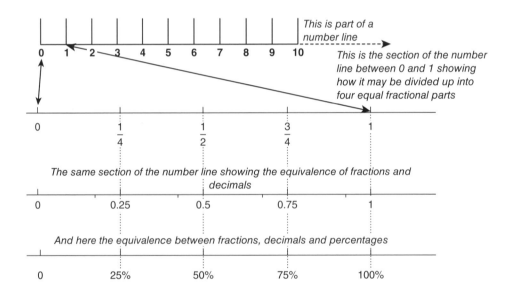

This is part of a number line

This is the section of the number line between 0 and 1 showing how it may be divided up into four equal fractional parts

The same section of the number line showing the equivalence of fractions and decimals

And here the equivalence between fractions, decimals and percentages

In the following explanations you will need to remember that a factor is a number that will divide into another number. For example, 3 is a factor of 6; 2 is a factor of 10.

Fractions

(i) A simple fraction, e.g. $\frac{3}{5}$, has a numerator (the top number) and a denominator (the bottom number). Both the numerator and the denominator will be whole numbers.

(ii) $\frac{3}{5}$ means 3 parts out of 5, or 3 divided by 5, or 3 shared by 5 or 3 lots of a fifth, or a fifth of 3. They all equal 3 ÷ 5, which is 0.6. Why? Think about a short division calculation:

$$\begin{array}{r} 0.6 \\ 5\overline{)3.^30} \end{array}$$ 5 into 3 doesn't go (goes 'o' times); there is a 'carry over' (a remainder) of 3.

5 into 30 goes 6. So the answer is 0.6

But of course with a calculator the calculation is easy and straightforward: $3 \div 5 = 0.6$

(iii) Equivalent fractions are formed by multiplying (or dividing) both the numerator and the denominator of a given fraction by the same number. For example:

$\dfrac{3}{5} = \dfrac{6}{10}$ *multiplying* the numerator and denominator by 2;

$\dfrac{9}{15} = \dfrac{3}{5}$ *dividing* the numerator and denominator by 3 which is a common factor. This is called cancelling. If an answer requires a fraction in its simplest form, you may need to cancel. This is shown in the following question: [4]

In a year group of 72 children, 30 are boys. What fraction of the year group are boys? Give your answer in its lowest terms.

The fraction $\dfrac{\text{boys}}{\text{total}} =$

$\dfrac{30}{72}$ $\xrightarrow[\text{by 2 which is a common factor}]{\text{divide numerator and denominator}}$ $\dfrac{15}{36}$ $\xrightarrow[\text{by 3 which is a common factor}]{\text{divide numerator and denominator}}$ $\dfrac{5}{12}$

There is no common factor of 5 and 12 so this is the answer given in its lowest terms.

(iv) In the mental test when answering questions asking you to find a fraction of a quantity you will need to do some multiplication and division. For example:

Find $\dfrac{3}{5}$ of 225. Solution: $\dfrac{1}{5}$ of $225 = 45$ (Why? Divide 225 by 5 . . . $5\overline{)225}^{45}$)

so $\dfrac{3}{5} = 3 \times 45 = 135$

Remember to round answers if necessary and appropriate. For example, money will only have 2 decimal places and a number of people will always be a whole number.

Decimals

Decimals are fractions with denominators which are multiples of 10 or 100 or 1000 or . . .

Thus $\dfrac{4}{10}$ which is the same as $4 \div 10 = 0.4$, and $\dfrac{56}{1000}$ which is $56 \div 1000 = 0.056$.

For on-screen questions a good idea would be to turn a fraction into a decimal using the calculator and then do any multiplication, for example find $\dfrac{4}{5}$ of £48. $\dfrac{4}{5} = 0.8$ and

$0.8 \times £48 = £38.40$

Percentages

Percentages are fractions with denominators of 100 (per cent means per 100).

For example, 5% represents $\dfrac{5}{100}$ which is the same as 0.05. 75% represents $\dfrac{75}{100}$ and this equals 0.75.

When you are answering the on-screen questions you will have access to a simple four-function calculator. The calculator is not available for the mental questions and therefore you may find it helpful to adopt a different approach, based, for example on doubling and halving. Thus a mental question such as find 35% of £200 would be tackled by:

- **finding 10% and multiplying by 3 to give 30%**
- **then halving the 10% value to find 5%**
- **then adding the two answers together.**

Thus 10% of £200 = £20. Therefore 30% = £60 and 5% = £10.

Therefore 35% = £60 + £10 = £70.

To change a fraction into a percentage, first change it into a decimal and then multiply by 100. For example, $\frac{3}{8} = 0.375 = 37.5\%$.

Here are some common fractions, decimals and percentages.

You should learn these.

1%	$\frac{1}{100}$	0.01	(divide by 100)
5%	$\frac{1}{20}$	0.05	(divide by 20)
10%	$\frac{1}{10}$	0.1	(divide by 10)
$12\frac{1}{2}\%$	$\frac{1}{8}$	0.125	(divide by 8)
20%	$\frac{1}{5}$	0.2	(divide by 5)
25%	$\frac{1}{4}$	0.25	(divide by 4)
50%	$\frac{1}{2}$	0.5	(divide by 2)
75%	$\frac{3}{4}$	0.75	(divide by 4, multiply by 3)

Questions

1. Simplify these fractions, writing them in their lowest terms:

   (a) $\frac{24}{36}$ (b) $\frac{18}{30}$ (c) $\frac{75}{100}$ (d) $\frac{27}{45}$

2. Write these percentages as decimals:

   (a) 15%   (b) 36%   (c) 65%   (d) 2%

3. Work out without using a calculator:

   (a) 28 × 2.5   (b) 3 × 3.45   (c) 0.9 × 180   (d) 1.5 × 15

4. Calculate without using a calculator:

   (a) 40% of 240   (b) 75% of 120   (c) 25% of 36   (d) 80% of 60

5. Find:

   (a) $\frac{3}{4}$ of 60   (b) $\frac{5}{8}$ of 64   (c) $\frac{2}{5}$ of 120   (d) $\frac{3}{8}$ of 560

6. Write these fractions as percentages:

   (a) $\frac{3}{8}$ (b) $\frac{4}{5}$ (c) $\frac{11}{25}$ (d) $\frac{28}{35}$

7. Write these percentages as fractions in their lowest terms:

   (a) 85%   (b) 30%   (c) 64%   (d) 6%

Mean, median, mode and range

The *mean* is the average most people give if asked for an average – the mean is found by adding up all the values in the list and dividing this total by the number of values.

The *median* is the middle value when all the values in the list are put in size order. If there are two 'middle' values the median is the mean of these two.

The *mode* is the most common value.

The *range* is the difference between the highest value and the lowest value.

Example

This example should illustrate each of the four calculations.

The children in Class 6 gained the following marks in a test:

Boys	45	46	48	60	42	53	47	51
	54	54	49	48	47	53	48	45
Girls	45	47	47	55	46	53	54	63
	48	50	46	51	48	48		

(Continued)

(Continued)

Work out the mean, median, mode and range for the boys and girls and compare the distributions of the marks.

The calculation for the boys:

$$Mean: \frac{42+45+45+46+47+47+48+48+48+49+51+53+53+54+54+60}{16}$$

$$= 49 \text{ (to the nearest whole number)}$$

Median: there are 16 values, so the median is midway between the 8th and 9th values

$$= \frac{48+48}{2} = 48$$

The *mode* is 48.

The *range* is $60 - 42 = 18$.

Question

8. Now work out the values for the girls. Then compare the distributions.

2 | Mental arithmetic

Notes

The mathematics required in this part of the test should usually be straightforward. The content and skills likely to be tested are listed in the Introduction (see page 5). Look back at this to remind yourself.

Key point

When you are taking the test, listen for, and jot down, numbers that may give short cuts or ease the calculations, such as those that allow doubling and halving. For example, multiply by 100 then divide by 2 if you need to multiply by 50, or multiply by 100 and divide by 4 if you are multiplying by 25. To calculate percentages, first find 10% by dividing by 10 then double for 20% or divide by 2 for 5% and so on. Look back at the hints in the Introduction.

Remember

- Calculators are not allowed.
- Questions will be read out twice. When answering the questions in this section, ask someone to read each question out to you and then, without a pause, read out the question again.
- There should then be a pause to allow you to record the answer before the next question is read out. The pause should be 18 seconds long.

Hint

You might find it helpful to ask someone to read out these practice questions. They will need to read them out at a sensible speed, as if they were reading a story to children. Remind them that each question should be read out twice and that they should then pause for 18 seconds, before reading out the next question. Numbers in these questions are in words, rather than using digits, to emphasise that they are spoken.

Questions

1. As part of a two and a quarter hour tennis training session, pupils received specialist coaching for one hour and twenty minutes. How many minutes of the training session remained?

(Continued)

(Continued)

2. A test has forty questions, each worth one mark. The pass mark was seventy per cent. How many questions had to be answered correctly to pass the test?

3. Dining tables seat six children. How many tables are needed to seat one hundred children?

4. Three classes of twenty-eight pupils took the end of Key Stage 2 mathematics test. Sixty-three pupils gained a scaled score of one hundred. What percentage is this?

5. A coach holds fifty-two passengers. How many coaches will be needed for a school party of four hundred and fifty people?

6. Eight kilometres is about five miles. About how many kilometres is thirty miles?

7. The journey from school to a sports centre took thirty-five minutes each way. The pupils spent two hours at the sports centre. They left school at oh-nine-thirty. At what time did they return?

8. It is possible to seat forty people in a row across the hall. How many rows are needed to seat four hundred and thirty-two people?

9. Pupils spent twenty-five hours in lessons each week. Four hours per week were allocated to science. What percentage of the lesson time per week was spent on the other subjects?

10. A science practical assessment contained two tasks. In the first task all fifteen members of a class scored four marks each. In the second task nine members scored five marks each and the other six members scored three marks each. What was the total number of marks scored by the class?

11. In a mock GCSE examination, eighty per cent of the pupils in class A achieved grade C and above. In class B twenty-two out of twenty-five pupils reached the same standard. What was the difference between the two classes in the percentage of pupils reaching grade C and above?

12. Two hundred pupils correctly completed a sponsored spell of fifty words. Each pupil was sponsored at five pence per word. How much money did the pupils raise in total?

13. A pupil scores forty-two marks out of a possible seventy in a class test. What percentage score is this?

14. There are one hundred and twenty pupils in a year group. Each has to take home two notices. Paper costs three pence per copy. How much will the notices cost?

15. What is seven and a half per cent as a decimal?

16. In a class of thirty-five pupils, four out of seven are boys. How many girls are there in the class?

17. In a school there are five classes of twenty-five pupils and five classes of twenty-eight pupils. How many pupils are there in the school?

18. A school has four hours and twenty-five minutes class contact time per day. What is the weekly contact time (assume a five-day week)?

19. In part one of an examination, a pupil scored eighteen marks out of a possible twenty-five marks. In part two he scored sixteen marks out of twenty-five. What was his final score for the examination? Give your answer as a percentage.

20. In a year group of one hundred and twenty pupils, eighty per cent achieved a grade four or a grade five in a mock GCSE English exam. Sixty pupils achieved a grade five. How many pupils achieved a grade four?

21. A part-time teacher has a contract to work for nought point four of the full-time equivalent contract per week. A full time week is five days. How many days per week would the teacher work?

22. In a year group of one hundred and forty-four pupils fifty-four pupils travel to school on school buses. What proportion of the year group does not travel on school buses? Give your answer as a decimal.

23. A space two point five metres by two point five metres is to be used for a flower bed. What is this area in square metres?

24. In a class of thirty pupils, sixty per cent of the pupils are girls. How many boys are there in the class?

25. A teacher takes pupils in the school minibus forty miles to the regional hockey trials. He estimates travelling at an average speed of twenty-five miles per hour. How many minutes will the journey take?

26. Twenty per cent of the pupils in a school with three hundred and fifteen pupils have free school meals. How many pupils is this?

27. In a practical assessment lasting one hour and twenty minutes a teacher allocated twenty minutes for setting up apparatus. What fraction of the lesson time was available for the actual assessment?

28. A class of twenty-four students takes GCSE French. The proportion of the class achieving grades A or A* is twelve and a half per cent. How many students achieve grades A or A*?

29. Three-fifths of a class of thirty-five pupils are boys. How many are girls?

30. In an end-of-year test nineteen pupils out of a class of twenty-five pupils gained half marks or more. What percentage of pupils gained less than half-marks?

31. What is twelve and one half per cent as a decimal?

32. What is four point zero five six multiplied by one hundred?

33. Two-fifths of pupils starting secondary school in September did not speak English as their first language. What percentage of the pupils did speak English as their first language?

(Continued)

(Continued)

34. A bus journey starts at eight fifty-five. It lasts for forty minutes. At what time does it finish?

35. Twenty per cent of the pupils in Year ten play hockey. Twenty-five per cent play basketball. The rest play football. There are two hundred pupils in Year Ten. How many play football?

36. For a charity swim twenty-five pupils each swam ten lengths of a twenty-five metre swimming pool. What was the total distance they swam? Give your answer in kilometres.

37. Out of one hundred and forty-four pupils in Year eleven, forty-eight do not continue in full-time education. What proportion of Year eleven pupils does continue in full-time education. Give your answer as a fraction in its lowest terms.

38. A teacher travels from school to a training course. After the course is over she returns to school. The distance to the training venue is twenty-four miles and expenses are paid at a rate of forty pence per mile. How much will she receive?

39. In a year eleven tutor group of thirty pupils the proportion who planned to stay on into year twelve was nought point seven. How many pupils did not plan to stay on into year twelve?

40. For a practical task a science teacher needs twenty-five millilitres of liquid for each pupil. There are twenty pupils in the class. How many millimetres of liquid are needed?

41. A teacher prepares an activity for a group of thirty-one pupils. The activity requires the pupils to work in groups of no more than four. Each group will need two rulers. What is the maximum number of rulers required?

42. The cost of the coach for a class history visit was two hundred and twenty-four pounds. The coach company announces that prices will increase by fifteen per cent next year. How much should the school expect to pay for the coach next year?

43. To make a small bookcase in a design class fifteen pupils each needed two point five metres of wood. The wood costs four pounds per metre. What was the total cost of providing the wood for the pupils?

44. A school group stays in Germany for two nights. The cost of accommodation for each member of the group is fifty-five euros per night. The exchange rate is one pound equals one point one euros. What is the cost of the accommodation in pounds for each member?

45. In a school's language GCSE course, pupils had to choose one language. One half chose French, one third chose German and the rest chose Chinese. What fraction of the pupils chose to study Chinese?

3 | Solving written arithmetic problems

Notes

Many of the questions in the skills test will require you to be able to interpret charts, tables and graphs. These are usually straightforward but do make sure that you read the questions thoroughly and read the tables or graphs carefully so that you will be able to identify the correct information. These questions are so varied that it is difficult to give examples for all of them – practice makes perfect, though.

There are some questions for which you may wish to revise the mathematics.

Fractions and percentages

See the brief notes in Chapter 1 for the essential knowledge. If you have to calculate percentage increases (or decreases), the simplest method is: find the actual difference, divide by the original amount and then multiply by 100 to convert this fraction to a percentage.

> #### Example
>
> Last year 30 pupils gained a level 3 in the National Tests. This year 44 gained a level 3. Calculate the percentage increase.
>
> Actual increase = 14.
>
> Percentage increase = $\dfrac{14}{30} \times 100 = 46.667\%$.
>
> (But note the comment below on rounding.)

Rounding

Clearly this answer, 46.667%, is too accurate. It would be better written as 46.7% (written to one decimal place) or as 47% (to the nearest whole number). You need to be able to round answers to a given number of decimal places or to the nearest whole number (depending on what the question is demanding). The simple rule is that if the first digit that you wish to remove is 5 or more, then you add 1 to the last remaining digit in the answer. If the first digit is less than 5 then the digits are just removed.

Examples:

46.3	= 46 to the nearest whole number
0.345	= 0.35 to two decimal places
34.3478	= 34.348 to three decimal places
34.3478	= 34.35 to two decimal places

$$34.3478 \ = \ 34.3 \text{ to one decimal place}$$
$$34.3478 \ = \ 34 \text{ to the nearest whole number}$$

Ratio and proportion

These sorts of questions are best illustrated with examples:

Example

(a) Divide £60 between 3 people in the ratio 1:2:3.

The total number of 'parts' is $1 + 2 + 3 = 6$.

Therefore 1 part = £60 ÷ 6 = £10.

Therefore the money is shared as £10; £20; £30.

(b) Four times as many children in a class have school dinners as do not. If there are 30 children, how many have school dinners?

The ratio is 4:1 giving $4 + 1 = 5$ parts. Therefore 1 'part' = 30 ÷ 5 = 6. Therefore $4 \times 6 = 24$ children have school dinners.

Don't confuse ratio and proportion. Ratio is 'part to part' while proportion is 'part to whole' and is usually given as a fraction. If the question asked 'What proportion of children have school dinners?' the answer would be $\frac{24}{30} = \frac{4}{5}$.

Notes on measures

You need to know and be able to change between the main metric units of measurement. For example:

Length   1 kilometre = 1000 metres
            1 metre = 100 centimetres or 1000 millimetres
            1 centimetre = 10 millimetres

Mass   1 kilogram = 1000 grams
            1 tonne = 1000 kilograms

Capacity 1 litre = 1000 millilitres = 100 centilitres

Notes on algebra

Generally a formula will be given to you, either in words or letters, and you will need to substitute numbers into that formula and arrive at an answer through what will be essentially an arithmetic rather than algebraic process. Remember the rules that tell you the order in which you should work through calculations.

- Brackets should be evaluated first.
- Then work out the multiplications and divisions.
- Finally work out the additions and subtractions.

Thus:　(i)　$2 \times 3 + 4 = 6 + 4 = 10$, but $2 + 3 \times 4 = 14$ (i.e. $2 + 12$) not 20

(ii)　$\dfrac{6+4}{2} = \dfrac{10}{2} = 5$

Here do not divide the 6 by 2 which would give $3 + 4 = 7$ or the 4 by 2 which would give $6 + 2 = 8$.

(iii)　$2(3 + 6) = 2 \times 9 = 18$

Note that some of the questions which follow have several parts. This is to save space in this text. In the actual test each 'part' would be a separate question. Thus question 1, for example, could appear as 4 different questions all using the same information. One question would be to calculate the mean, one the median, one the mode and one the range.

Questions

1. There were 30 pupils in a class. Their results in a test are summarised in the table below.

Mark out of 40	Number of pupils achieving mark
19	2
24	8
27	1
29	5
33	2
34	5
36	7

What are the mean, mode and range for these results?

2. A teacher was planning a school trip to Germany. Each pupil was to be allowed €100 spending money. At the time she planned the trip £1 was equivalent to €1.14. How much English money did each pupil need to exchange in order to receive €100?

(Continued)

(*Continued*)

3. Five times as many pupils in a school obtained a scaled score of 100 in the Key Stage 2 mathematics test as obtained a score of 101. No pupil scored less than 100. If a total of 32 pupils took the test and just two pupils scored more than 101 how many pupils scored 100?

4. Teachers in a mathematics department analysed the Key Stage 2 National Test results for mathematics from three feeder schools.

Scaled score	School A Number of pupils	School B Number of pupils	School C Number of pupils	Totals
98	5	3	4	12
99	6	8	8	22
100	16	18	15	49
101	6	3	8	17
Totals	33	32	35	

Which school had the greatest percentage of pupils with a score of 100 and above?

5. The national percentage of pupils with SEN (including statements) is about 18%. A school of 250 pupils has 35 children on the SEN register. How many children is this below the national average?

6. A secondary school analysed its GCSE results for French for the period 2013–16. The table shows the number of pupils at each grade:

French	Grade A	Grade B	Grade C	Grade D or lower
2016	19	15	7	1
2015	14	18	3	
2014	23	21	4	
2013	21	16	5	6

Which of the following statements is correct?

A   The percentage of pupils gaining grade A or grade B in 2013 was greater than in 2016.

B   The percentage of pupils who failed to gain a grade A was greater in 2015 than in 2014.

C   The percentage of pupils gaining grade A in 2016 was approximately 5 percentage points higher than in 2015.

7. An end of year assessment for a class of 27 Year 10 pupils was planned to take 6 hours. As part of the assessment each pupil required access to a computer for 25% of the time. The school's ICT suite contained 30 computers and could be booked for a number of 40-minute sessions.

How many computer sessions needed to be booked for the class?

8. A pupil achieved a mark of 58 out of 75 for practical work and 65 out of 125 on the written paper. The practical mark was worth 60% of the final mark and the written paper 40% of the final mark. The minimum mark required for each grade is shown below.

Grade	Minimum mark
A*	80%
A	65%
B	55%
C	45%
D	35%

What was the grade achieved by this pupil?

9. A pupil obtained the following marks in three tests.

In which test did the pupil do best?

Test 1	Test 2	Test 3
$\frac{45}{60}$	$\frac{28}{40}$	$\frac{23}{30}$

10. A school has a target that at least $\frac{2}{3}$ of the pupils in a class should have parents or carers coming to parents' evenings.

A week before the Year 7 parents' evening a deputy head compiled this table:

Class	Number in class	Number of pupils with parents/carers attending
7SW	25	15
7MP	27	17
7PH	31	23
7TS	32	20
7TM	29	24

Which classes are not meeting the school's target?

(Continued)

(Continued)

11. The scores for a group of pupils in a series of English tests are shown below:

Pupil	Test 1	Test 2	Test 3	Test 4	Test 5
A	19	13	15	17	11
B	6	9	5	10	15
C	13	14	11	13	14
D	18	12	20	12	18

Indicate all the true statements:

A   The highest mean score by a pupil is 16.

B   Pupil B has the greatest range of test scores.

C   All pupils scored more in Test 5 than in Test 1.

12. A teacher analysed the number of pupils in a school achieving level 4 and above in the end of Key Stage 2 English tests for 2011–14.

	Year			
	2011	2012	2013	2014
Pupils achieving level 4 and above	70	74	82	84
Pupils in year group	94	98	104	110

In each year the school was set a target of 75% of pupils to achieve a level 4 or above in the end of Key Stage 2 English tests.

(a) By how many percentage points did the school exceed its target in 2014? Give your answer to the nearest whole number.

(b) In which year was the target exceeded by the greatest margin?

13. A primary school teacher records the difference between the reading ages and actual ages of the 30 pupils in her class, grouping the results together. The table shows that, for example, there are 3 boys whose reading ages are more than 3 years and up to 6 years below their actual ages.

Difference, d, between reading age and actual age in months d = (reading age – actual age)	Number of pupils	
	Boys	Girls
$-9 < d \le -15$	1	1
$-6 < d \le -9$	3	1
$-3 < d \le -6$	3	
$0 < d \le -3$	2	2

Difference, d, between reading age and actual age in months d = (reading age – actual age)	Number of pupils	
	Boys	Girls
0		2
$0 < d \le +3$	3	1
$+3 < d \le +6$	1	3
$+6 < d \le +9$	1	3
$+9 < d \le +15$	1	2

Indicate all the true statements:

A   More boys than girls have reading ages below their actual ages.

B   The proportion of girls with a reading age greater than their actual age is 0.6.

C   Three pupils have a reading age of 1 year or more above their actual age.

14. Four schools had the following proportion of pupils with SEN.

School	Proportion
P	$\frac{2}{9}$
Q	0.17
R	57 out of 300
S	18%

Which school had the lowest proportion of pupils with SEN?

A School P   B School Q   C School R   D School S

15. This table shows the marks gained by a group of pupils in Year 3 in a mathematics test.

Pupil	Marks	Pupil	Marks
A	36	K	56
B	62	L	54
C	64	M	32
D	42	N	35
E	46	O	67
F	50	P	58
G	63	Q	63
H	68	R	60
I	39	S	62
J	61	T	58

(Continued)

(Continued)

The school will use the results to predict their levels for mathematics at the end of Year 6, and will target those pupils who, it is predicted, will achieve scaled scores of less than 100 in the Year 6 tests.

This is the conversion chart the school uses to change marks to expected scaled scores:

Mark range	<40	40–59	60–64	65 and over
Expected scaled score	85–94	95–99	100	101–120

How many pupils will be targeted?

16. A school has analysed the results of its students at GCSE and A level for several years and from these produced a graph which it uses to predict the average A level points score for a given average points score at GCSE.

    Use the graph below to predict the points score at A level if the GCSE points score were 6.

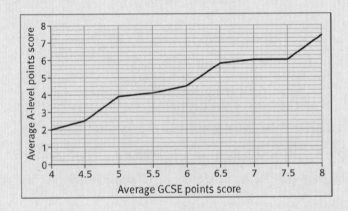

17. A junior school has a weekly lesson time of 23.5 hours. Curriculum analysis gives the following amount of time to the core subjects:

English:	6 hours 30 mins
Mathematics:	5 hours
Science:	1 hour 30 mins

    Calculate the percentage of curriculum time given to English. Give your answer to the nearest per cent.

18. A support teacher assessed the reading ages of a group of 10 Year 8 pupils with SEN.

Pupil	Actual age		Reading age	
	Years	Months	Years	Months
A	12	07	10	08
B	12	01	11	09
C	12	03	9	07
D	12	03	13	06
E	12	01	10	02
F	12	11	12	00
G	12	06	8	04
H	12	07	10	00
I	12	06	11	08
J	12	02	10	10

What percentage of the 10 pupils had a reading age of at least 1 year 6 months below the actual age?

19. A teacher analysed pupils' performance at the end of Year 5 in 2015.

Pupils judged to have achieved level 3 and below were targeted for extra support.

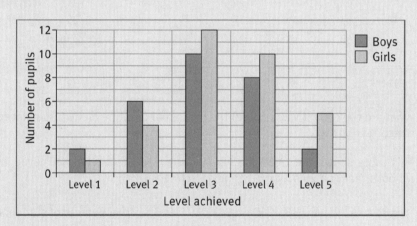

What fraction of the pupils needed extra support?

20. A plastic drinking cup has a capacity of 100ml.

How many cups could be filled from a 1.5 litre carton of juice?

21. A teacher recorded the number of laps of a rectangular field walked by pupils in Years 5 and 6 in a school's annual walk for charity.

(Continued)

(Continued)

Year group	Number of pupils	Number of laps
5	65	8
6	94	10

The rectangular field measured 200 metres by 150 metres.

The teacher calculated the total distance covered.

Which of the following shows the total distance in kilometres?

A 1022   B 1460   C 10220   D 111.3

22. A primary teacher required each pupil to have a piece of card measuring 20cm by 45cm for a lesson. Large sheets of card measured 60cm by 50cm. What was the minimum number of large sheets of card required for a class of 28 pupils?

23. In a review of the test performance of three pupils a teacher prepares a table of their marks in a series of class tests.

	Percentage marks in each test					Mean mark	Median mark
Pupil	Test 1	Test 2	Test 3	Test 4	Test 5		
A	39	50	34	32	35	38	Place here
B	37	48	32	28	30	35	32
C	36	47	34	33	45	Place here	34

32		35		38		39

What are the correct values of (a) the median and (b) the mean to be placed in the correct boxes?

24. This table shows the GCSE grades in design and technology achieved by a school's Year 11 pupils for the period 2013 to 2016.

Grade	A*	A	B	C	D	E	F/G	Total number of students
2013	1	2	2	11	5	6	1	28
2014	6	5	9	13	1	0	0	34
2015	4	7	9	16	4	0	0	40
2016	5	6	8	10	4	2	1	36

Which of the following statements is correct?

A   2014 had the highest percentage of grades A and A*.

B   2015 had the lowest percentage of grade C.

C   Less than $\frac{1}{4}$ of pupils gained a grade B in any year.

25. Using the relationship 5 miles = 8km, convert:

    (a) 120 miles into kilometres;

    (b) 50km into miles.

    (Give your answers to the nearest whole number in each case.)

26. A ream of photocopier paper (500 sheets) is approximately 5cm thick. What is the approximate thickness of 1 sheet of paper? Give your answers in millimetres.

27. A teacher organised revision classes for pupils who achieved grades C and D in mock examinations and used the following table to assess the number of pupils who might benefit from attending the classes.

Grade	Boys	Girls	Total
A*	3	5	8
A	4	3	7
B	6	8	14
C	7	4	11
D	4	5	9
E	3	3	6
F	2	2	4
G	1	0	1

What percentage of the pupils would benefit from attending the classes?

Give your answer to the nearest whole number.

28. A piece of fabric measuring 32cm by 15cm was required for each pupil in a Year 8 design and technology lesson. What was the minimum length of 120cm wide fabric required for 29 pupils?

29. A school trip is organised from Derby to London – approximately 120 miles. A teacher makes the following assumptions.

    (a) The pupils will need a 30-minute break during the journey.

    (b) The coach will be able to average 40 miles an hour, allowing for roadworks and traffic.

    (c) The coach is due in London at 9 a.m.

    What would be the latest time for the coach to leave Derby?

30. A teacher organised a hike for a group of pupils during a school's activity week. The route was measured on a 1:50 000 scale map and the distances on the map for each stage of the hike were listed on the chart below.

(Continued)

(Continued)

Stage of hike	Distance on map (cm)
1. Start to Stop A	14.3
2. Stop A to Stop B	8.7
3. Stop B to Stop C	9.3

What was the total distance travelled on the hike?

Give your answer to the nearest kilometre.

31. The following table shows the time for 4 children swimming in a relay race.

1st length	John	95.6 seconds
2nd length	Karen	87.3 seconds
3rd length	Julie	91.3 seconds
4th length	Robert	89.4 seconds

What was the total time, in minutes and seconds, that they took?

32. A teacher completed the following expenses claim form after attending a training course.

Travelling From	To	Miles	Expenses
School and return	Training centre to school	238	Place here
Other expenses	Car parking		£7.50
	Evening meal		£10.50
		Total claim	Place here

The mileage rates were:

30p per mile for the first 100 miles

26p per mile for the remainder.

Complete the claim form by placing the correct values in the expenses column.

£40.88   £65.88   £71.38   £73.88   £83.88   £87.00   £89.40

33. A classroom assistant works from 9:00 a.m. until 12 noon for 4 days per week in a primary school and has a 15 minute break from 10:30 until 10:45. She provides learning support for pupils – each pupil receiving a continuous 20 minutes' session. How many pupils can she support each week?

34. The mean height of 20 girls in Year 7 is 1.51m. Another girl who is 1.6m joins the class. Calculate the new mean height.

35. A primary school teacher produces a table showing the differences between the reading age and the actual age for two tests for a group of 16 pupils.

Reading age minus actual age (months)

Test 1	Test 2
−10	−9
−9	−8
−7	−7
−7	−6
−5	−2
−2	0
0	0
0	2
3	4
3	3
3	6
6	7
7	8
9	9
9	10
10	10

(a) Which test had the greatest range in the values of 'reading age – actual age'?

(b) What proportion of pupils made no progress? Give your answer to one decimal place.

36. Equipment for a school is delivered in boxes 15cm deep. The boxes are to be stacked in a cupboard which is 1.24m high. How many layers of boxes will fit into the cupboard?

37. To inform planning a head of science produced a pie chart showing the subject choices made by 150 pupils entering the sixth form. How many more pupils chose to study maths than chose to study chemistry?

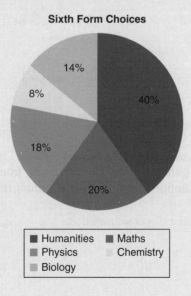

Sixth Form Choices

14%
8%
40%
18%
20%

Humanities   Maths
Physics   Chemistry
Biology

(Continued)

(Continued)

38. A teacher planned a school trip from Calais to a study centre. The distance from Calais to the centre is 400km. The coach is expected to travel at an average speed of 50 miles per hour, including time for breaks. The coach is due to leave Calais at 06:20. What time should it arrive at the study centre?

    Use the conversion rate of $1km = \frac{5}{8}mile$.

    Give your answer using the 24-hour clock.

39. The raw scores in a GCSE examination are converted to uniform marks (UMS) by using a graph, part of which is shown below.

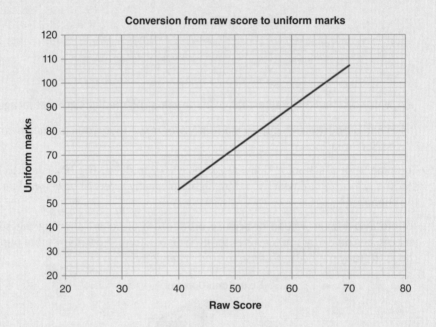

Uniform marks are then converted to grades using the following table of grade boundary marks:

Grade	A*	A	B	C	D	E	F
UMS	80	70	60	50	40	30	20

A student achieves a raw score of 52.

Select the grade that the student is awarded.

(a) A

(b) B

(c) C

40. Moderators sample the coursework marked by teachers in school. A moderator will select a sample from a school according to the guidelines and rules. One rule that fixes the size of the sample to be selected is:

Size(s) $= 10 + \dfrac{n}{10}$ where n is the number of candidates in a school.

What would be the sample size if there were 150 candidates?

41. A teacher prepared tables to show the relationship between GCSE English Language grades and GCSE Mathematics and French grades.

		GCSE Mathematics						GCSE French					
	GCSE Grade	A*–A	B–C	D–E	F–G	U–X	Total	A*–A	B–C	D–E	F–G	U–X	Total
GCSE English language	A*–A	7	23	8			38	10	6				16
	B–C	5	40	10	2		57	10	16	1			27
	D–E		9	6	7	3	25		17	14	1	1	33
	F–G								1	1	2		4
	U–X												
	Total	12	72	24	9	3	120	20	40	16	3	1	80

Indicate all the true statements:

A The grade A*–C pass rate for GCSE French was 5 percentage points higher than the A*–C pass rate for mathematics.

B Of the pupils taking GCSE mathematics, more than half achieved grade C or above in GCSE English language.

C Of the pupils taking GCSE French, one-third did not achieve grade C or above.

42. As part of a target-setting programme a teacher compared the marks for 10 pupils in each of 2 tests.

Pupils' marks out of 120

Pupil	Test 1	Test 2
A	70	66
B	61	68

(Continued)

(Continued)

Pupils' marks out of 120

Pupil	Test 1	Test 2
C	64	63
D	56	41
E	70	78
F	60	59
G	64	77
H	72	80
I	39	44
J	62	57

Write down the letters for those pupils who scored at least 5 percentage points more in test 2 than test 1.

Note: In the actual test this question would be expressed as 'Indicate by clicking anywhere on the rows which pupils scored at least 5 percentage points more in test 2 than test 1'.

43. A pupil achieved the following scores in Tests A, B and C.

Test	A	B	C
Actual mark	70	60	7

The pupil's weighted score was calculated using the following formula:

$$\text{Weighted score} = \frac{(A \times 60)}{100} + \frac{B \times 30}{80} + C$$

What was the pupil's weighted score?

Give your answer to the nearest whole number.

44. A teacher used a spreadsheet to calculate pupils' marks in a mock GCSE exam made up of two papers. Paper 1 was worth 25% of the total achieved and Paper 2 was worth 75% of the total achieved.

This table shows the first four entries in the spreadsheet.

	Paper 1 Mark out of 30	(25%) Weighted mark	Paper 2 Mark out of 120	(75%) Weighted mark	Final weighted mark
Pupil A	24	20	80	50	70
Pupil B	20	16.7	68	42.5	59.2
Pupil C	8	6.7	59	36.9	43.6
Pupil D	20	16.7	74	46.3	63

Pupil E scored 18 on Paper 1 and 64 on Paper 2.

What was the final weighted mark for Pupil E?

45. The table below shows the percentage test results for a group of pupils.

Pupil	Test 1	Test 2	Test 3	Test 4	Test 5	Test 6	Test 7	Test 8
A	92	85	87	82	78	26	92	95
B	53	70	72	38	15	27	83	73
C	61	77	69	68	60	30	90	77
D	95	100	93	30	92	30	100	70
E	72	49	47	42	46	82	72	92
F	58	78	38	46	34	58	98	78

Indicate all the true statements.

A   The greatest range of % marks achieved was in test 2.

B   Pupil C achieved a mean mark of 66.5%.

C   The median mark for test 6 was 30.

46. A single mark for a GCSE examination is calculated from three components using the following formula:

Final mark = Component A × 0.6 + Component B × 0.3 + Component C × 0.1

A candidate obtained the following marks.

Component A   64
Component B   36
Component C   40

What was this candidate's final mark? Give your answer to the nearest whole number.

47. A pupil submitted two GCSE coursework tasks, Task A and Task B. Task A carried a weighting of 60% and Task B a weighting of 40%. Each task was marked out of 100.

The pupil scored 80 marks in Task A.

What would be the minimum mark score required by the pupil in Task B to achieve an overall mark across the two tasks of 60%?

48. A reading test consists of 4 parts. The scores are added together to provide a raw score. The table below converts raw scores into an age-standardised reading score.

	Age in years and months							
	6.05	6.06	6.07	6.08	6.09	6.10	6.11	7.00
Raw score	Age-standardised reading score							
16	97	97	96	96	96	96	96	96
17	98	98	98	98	97	97	97	97
18	99	99	99	99	99	98	98	98
19	101	100	100	100	100	100	99	99
20	102	102	101	101	101	101	101	101

(Continued)

(Continued)

A pupil whose age is 6 years and 10 months obtained scores of 2, 5, 4 and 7 from the four parts of the test.

What was the pupil's age standardised reading score?

49. A teacher calculated the speed in kilometres per hour of a pupil who completed a 6km cross-country race.

Use the formula: Distance = speed × time.

The pupil took 48 minutes.

What was the pupil's speed in kilometres per hour?

50. A readability test for worksheets, structured examination questions, etc. uses the formula:

$$\text{Reading level} = 5 + \left\{ 20 - \frac{x}{15} \right\}$$

where x = the average number of monosyllabic words per 150 words of writing.

Calculate the reading level for a paper where x = 20. Give your answer correct to two decimal places.

51. To help pupils set individual targets a teacher calculated predicted A level points scores using the following formula:

$$\text{Predicted A level points score} = \left(\frac{\text{total GCSE points score}}{\text{number of GCSEs}} \times 3.9 \right) - 17.5$$

GCSE grades were awarded the following points.

GCSE grade	A*	A	B	C
Points	8	7	6	5

Calculate the predicted A level points score for a pupil who at GCSE gained 4 passes at grade C, 4 at grade B, 1 at grade A and 1 at grade A*.

52. A candidate's final mark in a GCSE examination is calculated from two components as follows:

Final mark = mark in component 1 × 0.6 + mark in component 2 × 0.4

A candidate needs a mark of 80 or more to be awarded a grade A*. If the mark awarded in component 2 was 70, what would be the lowest mark needed in component 1 to gain a grade A*?

53. A PGCE student looks at the Ofsted report for a secondary school which is advertising for a teacher in humanities.

Subject	Number of entries	% A*–A	% A*–C	% A*–G	% ungraded
History	80	35	85	98	2
Geography	60	20	65	95	5
Sociology	25	40	52	92	8
Psychology	28	35	55	100	0
English	166	42	80	99	1

Indicate all the true statements:

A   28 of the History students achieved an A* or an A grade.
B   More students were ungraded in Sociology than in Geography.
C   In English twice as many students gained an A*–C grade as gained an A*–A grade.

54. In the annual sports day at a school pupils took part in a running race or in a field event or both. Pupils who took part in both were given an award. In Years 5 and 6 all 72 pupils took part in a running race or in a field event or both. $\frac{1}{2}$ took part in a running race and $\frac{3}{4}$ took part in a field event. How many pupils were given an award?

55. A school used the ALIS formula relating predicted A level points scores to mean GCSE points scores for A level mathematics pupils. The formula used was:

Predicted A level points score = (mean GCSE points score × 2.24) − 7.35

What was the predicted A level points score for a pupil with a mean GCSE points score of 7.55? Give your answer correct to one decimal place.

56. To inform a discussion on target setting, a head teacher compared the GCSE grades of pupils from schools in the same area.

Percentage of pupils achieving 5 or more A*–C grades

Year	School A	School B	School C	School D
2013	51	57	53	57
2014	53	60	54	62
2015	53	73	62	66
2016	56	81	66	69

Indicate all the true statements:

(Continued)

(Continued)

A   All the schools had an annual increase in the percentage of pupils achieving five or more A*–C grades over the four-year period.

B   Over the four-year period, school B had the greatest increase in the percentage of pupils achieving five or more A*–C grades.

C   In 2016, there was a 12 percentage points difference between the two highest achieving schools.

57. An English department organised a trip to the theatre for 35 pupils. The cost of the coach was £280 and the cost of the tickets was £8 per pupil. The school contributed part of the total cost. Each pupil paid £12. What fraction of the total cost was contributed by the school?

58. There were 27 pupils in a Year 8 history class.

    One pupil was absent when there was a mid-term test. The mean score for the group was 56.

    On returning to school the pupil who had been absent took the test and scored 86.

    What was the revised mean test score?

    Give your answer correct to one decimal place.

59. A school report includes the school's grades for each pupil's attainment in each subject.

    Grade A is awarded for an average test mark of 75% and above.

    The table below shows the results for an English test for a group of 24 pupils.

Pupil	Mark	Pupil	Mark
A	31	M	7
B	34	N	15
C	12	O	31
D	17	P	23
E	29	Q	26
F	19	R	28
G	24	S	29
H	30	T	33
I	32	U	29
J	28	V	34
K	25	W	30
L	33	X	28

    If the test was marked out of 36, how many pupils achieved a grade A?

60. An art teacher plans to take a group of 66 GCSE pupils together with a number of accompanying adults to an art gallery and museum.

    The admission charges are as follows.

	Adults	Students
Art gallery	£8.50	£4.50
Museum	£5.50	£3.50
Combined ticket	£12.00	£6.00

One adult is admitted free when accompanying 30 students.

The group visits both the art gallery and the museum.

(a) How much is saved on the total student admission costs by buying combined tickets?

The school requires a ratio of at least 1 adult for every 20 students on educational visits.

(b) What is the cost of the combined tickets for the adults taking into account the free places they will get?

61. A teacher is planning a visit to an activity centre with a group of students. They will use the school minibus.

The round trip is approximately 200 miles. The fuel consumption for the minibus is 32 miles per gallon. The minibus uses diesel fuel which costs £1.34 per litre.

1 gallon = 4.546 litres

What is the estimated fuel cost for the visit? Give your answer to the nearest pound.

62. To inform a staff meeting a teacher prepared a table comparing pupils' results in English, maths and science in mock GCSE examinations.

120 boys and 112 girls took the mock examinations.

Subject		Number of pupils achieving at grades 5–7		
		Grade 5	Grade 6	Grade 7
English	Boys	20	48	32
	Girls	10	48	40
Mathematics	Boys	20	56	32
	Girls	12	52	32
Science	Boys	20	56	36
	Girls	16	52	32

(a) In which subject was the percentage of boys achieving grade 6 and above greater than the percentage of girls achieving grade 6 and above?

(b) What proportion of pupils did not achieve a grade 5 or above in English in the tests? Give your answer as a decimal to two decimal places.

4 | Interpreting and using written data

Notes

You will not be required to draw tables or plot graphs when answering written data questions. The following notes are intended to give you a brief summary of some aspects, including terms and representations that may be unfamiliar.

Some of the information received by schools, for example, analyses of pupil performance, uses 'cumulative frequencies' or 'cumulative percentages'. One way to illustrate cumulative frequencies is through an example. The table shows the marks gained in a test by the 60 pupils in a year group.

22	13	33	31	51	24	37	83	39	28
31	64	23	35	9	34	42	26	68	38
63	34	44	77	37	15	38	54	34	22
47	25	48	38	53	52	35	45	32	31
37	43	37	49	24	17	48	29	57	33
30	36	42	36	43	38	39	48	39	59

We could complete a tally chart and a frequency table.

Mark, m	Tally	Frequency
9	1	1
10	0	0
11	0	0
12	0	0
13	1	1
and so on		

But 60 results are a lot to analyse and we could group the results together in intervals. A sensible interval in this case would be a band of 10 marks. This is a bit like putting the results into 'bins'.

	13	22	33		
		24	31, 37		
		28	39		
$0 \leq m < 10$	$10 \leq m < 20$	$20 \leq m < 30$	$30 \leq m < 40$	$40 \leq m < 50$	etc.

Note that $\leq$ means 'less than or equal to' and $<$ means 'less than', so $30 \leq m < 40$ means all the marks between 30 and 40 including 30 but excluding 40.

Here are the marks grouped into a frequency table.

Mark, m	Frequency	Cumulative frequency
$0 \leq m < 10$	1	1
$10 \leq m < 20$	3	4
$20 \leq m < 30$	9	13
$30 \leq m < 40$	25	38
$40 \leq m < 50$	11	49
$50 \leq m < 60$	6	55
$60 \leq m < 70$	3	58
$70 \leq m < 80$	1	59
$80 \leq m < 90$	1	60

Note how the cumulative frequency is calculated:

← 4 = 1 + 3

← 13 = 1 + 3 + 9, i.e. 4 + 9

← 38 = 1 + 3 + 9 + 25, i.e. 13 + 25

The last column 'Cumulative frequency' gives the 'running total' – in this case the number of pupils with less than a certain mark. For example, there are 38 pupils who gained less than 40 marks.

The values for cumulative frequency can be plotted to give a cumulative frequency curve as shown below.

Note that the cumulative frequency values are plotted at the right-hand end of each interval, i.e. at 10, 20, 30 and so on.

You can use a cumulative frequency curve to estimate the median mark: the median for any particular assessment is the score or level which half the relevant pupils exceed and half do not achieve.

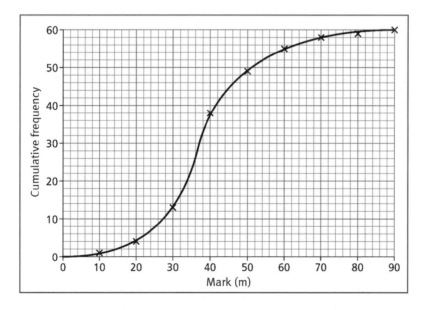

There are 60 pupils, so the median mark will be the 30th mark. (Find 30 on the vertical scale and go across the graph until you reach the curve and read off the value on the horizontal scale.) The median mark is about 37 – check that you agree.

It is also possible to find the quartiles. These are described in the Glossary on page 94.

The lower quartile will be at 25% of 60, that is the 15th value, giving a mark of about 31; the upper quartile is at 75% of 60, thus the 45th value, giving a mark of about 45.

The diagram below should further help to explain these terms. It also helps to introduce the idea of a 'box and whisker' plot.

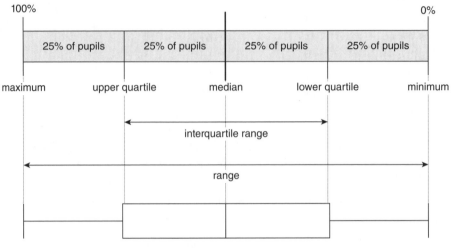

Box and whisker plot

The 'whiskers' indicate the maximum and minimum values, the ends of the 'box' the upper quartile and the lower quartile, and the median is shown by the line drawn across the inside of the box. The 'middle 50%' of the values lie within the box and only the top 25% and the bottom 25% are outside the box.

Questions

1. A secondary school has compared performance in the Key Stage 2 National Tests with performance at GCSE. The comparison is shown on the graph below.

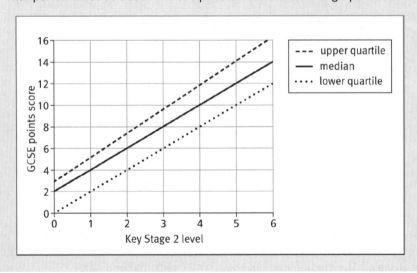

(a) What is the median GCSE points score of those pupils scoring a 2 at Key Stage 2?

(b) A pupil had a Key Stage 2 score of 5 and a GCSE points score of 11. Is it true to say that he was likely to be within the bottom 25% of all pupils?

(c) Is it true that 50% of the pupils who gained level 4 at Key Stage 2 gained GCSE points scores within the range 8 to 12?

2. To assist a discussion at a department meeting the head of mathematics pre-pared a box-and-whisker diagram of the end-of-year test results for the four maths classes in Year 10. Each class has 28 pupils.

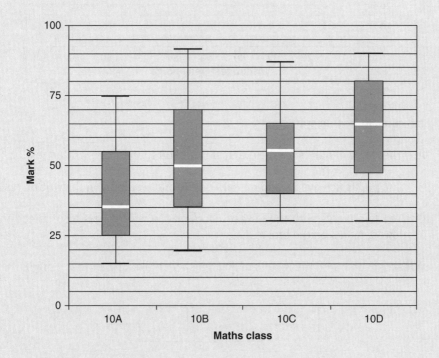

Indicate all the true statements:

A   The highest % mark was achieved in class 10B.

B   In each class 21 or more pupils achieved at least 40%.

C   The range of % marks in class 10A and class 10D was the same.

3. A German language teacher compared the results of a German oral test and a German written test given to a group of 16 pupils.

(Continued)

(Continued)

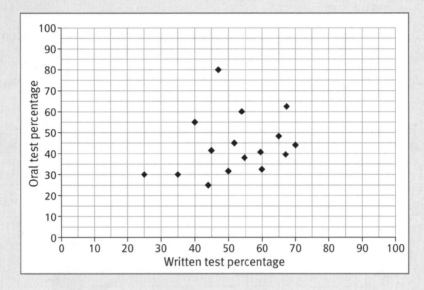

Indicate all the true statements.

A The range of marks for the oral test is greater than for the written test.

B $\frac{1}{4}$ of pupils achieved a higher mark on the oral test than on the written test.

C The two pupils with the lowest marks on the written test also gained the lowest marks on the oral test.

4. A teacher compared the results of an English test taken by all Year 8 pupils.

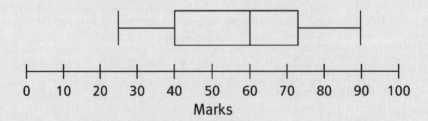

Indicate all the true statements.

A $\frac{1}{4}$ of all pupils scored more than 70 marks.

B $\frac{1}{2}$ of all pupils scored less than 60 marks.

C The range of marks was 65.

5. In 2016 a survey was made of the nightly TV viewing habits of 10-year-old children in town A and town B. The findings are shown in the pie charts below:

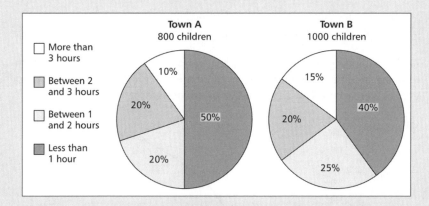

Use these pie charts to identify which of the following statements is true.

A   More children in town A watched TV for less than 1 hour than in town B.

B   More children in town B watched for between 2 and 3 hours than in town A.

C   100 children watched more than 3 hours in town A.

6. A teacher kept a box and whisker diagram to profile the progress of her class in practice tests. There are 16 pupils in the class.

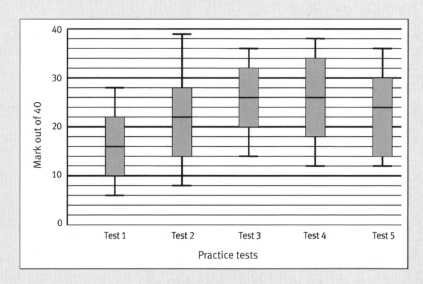

(a) In which test did 12 students achieve 20 or more marks?

(b) Indicate all the true statements.

(Continued)

(Continued)

    A   The highest mark was achieved in test 2.

    B   The median mark increased with each test.

    C   The range of marks in test 3 and test 4 was the same.

7. At the beginning of Year 11 pupils at a school took an internal test which was used to predict GCSE grades in mathematics. From the results the predicted grades were plotted on a cumulative frequency graph.

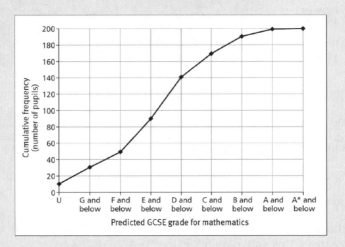

Indicate the true statement.

    A   30% of the pupils were predicted to achieve grade C.

    B   85% of the pupils were predicted to achieve grade C.

    C   15% of the pupils were predicted to achieve grade C.

8. This bar chart shows the amount of pocket money children in Year 7 receive.

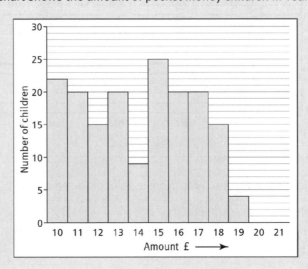

(a) How many children were surveyed?

(b) What is the modal amount of pocket money received?

9. A teacher recorded the marks given to five pupils in a series of mental arithmetic tests. Each test was based on 25 questions with 1 mark awarded for each correct answer.

Pupil	Test 1	Test 2	Test 3	Test 4
V	16	16	17	18
W	15	17	16	19
X	14	16	18	18
Y	16	17	18	18
Z	11	13	15	17

Indicate all the true statements.

A The marks for all the pupils increased steadily

B Pupil Z could be expected to gain a mark of 19 in the next test.

C The mean, the median and the mode have the same value for test 4.

10. A Year 7 teacher was given information from feeder primary schools about pupils in the tutor group.

The two box plots below show the reading scores for two feeder schools A and B.

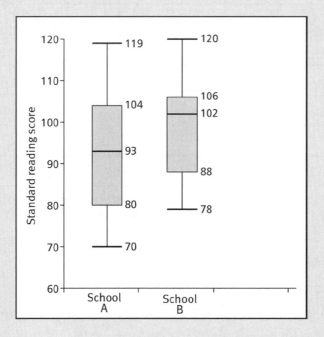

(Continued)

(Continued)

A standard reading score of 100 shows that a pupil's reading score was exactly on the national average for pupils of the same age. Standard scores of more than 100 show above average reading scores and below 100 show below average reading scores for pupils of the same age.

Indicate all the true statements.

A   The difference in the median scores for the two feeder schools was 9.

B   The interquartile range of the scores for school B was 18.

C   The range of scores was 9 less for school B than for school A.

11. Use the box plots and the information from question 10 to indicate the true statements.

A   50% of the pupils in school A had a reading score of 93 or more.

B   25% of pupils in school B scored 88 or less.

C   The interquartile range for the two schools was the same.

12. A mathematics teacher prepared a scatter graph to compare the results of pupils' performance in two tests. There were 24 pupils in the class.

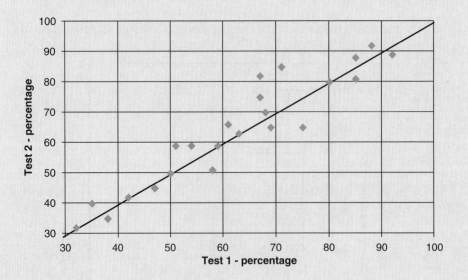

Indicate all the true statements.

A   6 pupils showed no improvement between the two tests.

B   A pupil who scored 71 in test 1 showed the greatest improvement in test 2.

C   9 pupils gained a lower percentage in test 2 than in test 1.

13. A teacher compared the results of pupils in a school's end of Key Stage 2 mathematics tests.

Results in mathematics	Mean points scored per pupil		
	2011	2012	2013
Boys	22.5	23.2	24.5
Girls	24.3	24.8	25.6

Difference between boys' and girls' mean mathematics points scores			Mean difference for three-year period 2011–2013
2011	2012	2013	
1.8		1.1	

Write down:

(a) the difference between the boys' and girls' mean mathematics points scores for 2012;

(b) the mean difference for the three-year period 2011–2013.

Note: In the actual test this question could be worded: 'Place the correct values in the shaded boxes for:

- *the difference between the boys' and girls' mean mathematics points scores for 2012; and*

- *the mean difference for the three-year period 2011–2013.*

14. This box and whisker diagram shows the GCSE results in four subjects for a school in 2013.

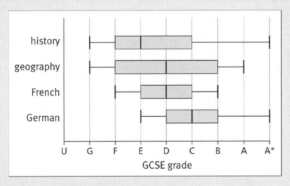

Indicate all the true statements.

A   50% of the pupils who took history gained grades F to C.

B   French had the lowest median grade.

C   50% of the pupils who took German gained grades C to A*.

(Continued)

(Continued)

15. The marks of ten students in the two papers of a German examination were plotted on this scatter graph:

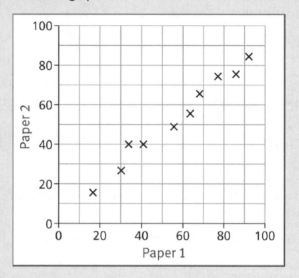

A student scored 53 marks on Paper 1 but missed Paper 2. What would you esti-mate her mark to be on Paper 2?

16. The straight line shows the mean levels scored in Year 9 assessments for a school plotted against the total GCSE points scores. The points A, B, C, D show the achievement of four pupils.

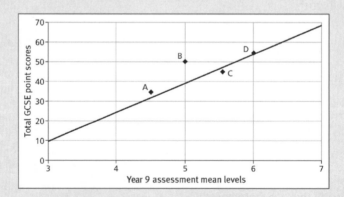

Indicate all the true statements.

A   Pupil D achieved as well as might have been predicted at GCSE.

B   Pupil C achieved a higher level in the Year 9 assessments than Pupil B but scored fewer points at GCSE than Pupil B.

C   At GCSE Pupil B achieved better than might have been predicted but Pupil A achieved less well than might have been predicted.

17. A teacher monitored the marks given to a group of four pupils in a series of spelling tests. Each test was based on spelling 20 words, with 1 mark given for each word spelt correctly.

Pupil	Test 1	Test 2	Test 3	Test 4
W	5	7	6	9
X	4	6	8	10
Y	6	7	8	9
Z	3	5	7	9

The trend of improvement for the pupils is expected to continue.

Which pupil would be expected to get a mark of 11 in the next test?

18. 20 pupils in a class took Test A at the beginning of a term and Test B at the end of the term.

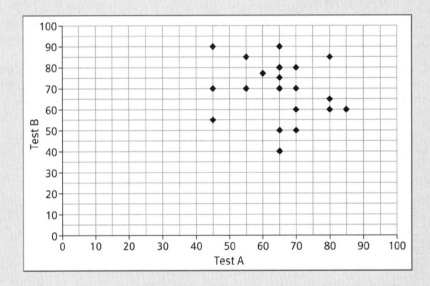

Indicate all the true statements.

A   The range of marks was wider for Test A than for Test B.

B   The lowest mark in Test A was lower than the lowest mark in Test B.

C   40% of the pupils scored the same mark or lower in Test B than in Test A.

D   More pupils scored over 60% in Test A than in Test B.

(Continued)

(Continued)

19. A teacher analysed the reading test standardised scores of a group of pupils.

Pupil	Gender	Age 8+ test standardised score	Age 10+ test standardised score
A	F	100	108
B	M	78	89
C	M	88	92
D	M	110	102
E	F	102	110
F	F	88	84
G	M	119	128
H	F	80	84

Indicate all the true statements.

A   All the girls improved their standardised scores between the Age 8+ and the Age 10+ tests.

B   The greatest improvement between the Age 8+ and the Age 10+ tests was achieved by a boy.

C $\frac{1}{4}$ of all the pupils had lower standardised scores in the Age 10+ tests than in the Age 8+ tests.

20. The Head of Year 11 conducted a survey of the amount of time pupils spent doing homework in a week. At a staff meeting to discuss pupil support for GCSE preparation a cumulative frequency graph of the results of the survey was shown.

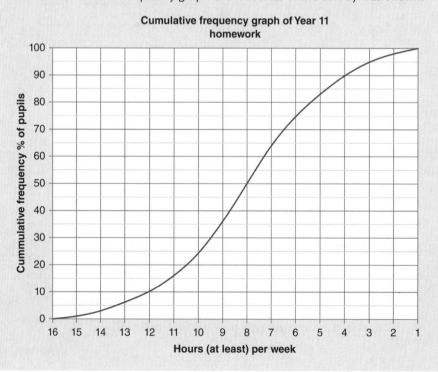

Cumulative frequency graph of Year 11 homework

Indicate all the true statements:

A   The median time spent on homework was 8 hours.

B   All pupils spent at least 1 hour doing homework during the week.

C   Three-quarters of the pupils spent at least 6 hours doing homework during the week.

21. Schools in a federation analysed the percentages of pupils gaining 5 A*–C grades in their GCSE examinations over a six-year period. The results are shown in this table.

Percentage of pupils gaining 5 A*–C grades

School	2009	2010	2011	2012	2013	2014
A	47.9	48.6	54.7	54.6	55.8	58.4
B	64.5	64.8	65.0	65.2	65.4	65.6
C	66.1	65.3	64.3	63.7	63.5	63.0
D	49.7	54.7	57.0	63.6	63.7	63.8
E	58.3	59.1	58.5	59.3	58.7	59.5

Which schools improved each year over the six-year period?

22. A research project compared the performance of Year 9 pupils taught mathematics, science and English in mixed classes or in single-sex classes.

This table shows the results.

Median level achieved

Subject	Boys only classes	Girls only classes	Mixed classes
English	7	8	8
Mathematics	7	8	7
Science	7	7	6

Indicate all the true statements.

A   The single-sex groups produced better results in science.

B   The mixed classes produced better results in English.

C   In mathematics, girls only classes achieved higher scores than the mixed classes.

(Continued)

(Continued)

23. At a staff meeting teachers were shown a table showing the proportion of pupils achieving at least half marks in the end of Year 9 tests.

Proportion of pupils achieving at least half marks in:	Year			
	2013 (%)	2014 (%)	2015 (%)	2016 (%)
English	75.8	76.3	75.8	76.5
Mathematics	69.6	70.2	70.8	71.4
Science	59.0	61.2	62.8	64.0

Indicate all the true statements:

A   The greatest year-on-year improvement was for science between 2013 and 2014.

B   All subjects achieved a year-on-year improvement over the four-year period.

C   The smallest improvement over the four-year period was for English.

24. For a department meeting a head of mathematics produced a box and whisker graph comparing the performance in the end of year tests of four classes in Year 7.

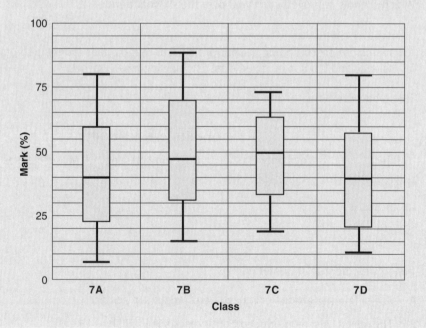

Indicate all the true statements.

A The lowest mark was scored by a pupil in class 7D.

B The median mark in class 7C was 10 marks higher than the median mark in class 7A.

C In class 7B one quarter of the pupils achieved a mark of 70% or more.

5 | Practice mental arithmetic and on-screen tests

Notes

Before you attempt the practice tests look back at the hints and advice on pages 2 and 3 and on page 13. If you want to time yourself remember the time limit is 48 minutes.

Practice mental arithmetic test

1. Three quarters of a year group of two hundred and forty pupils took part in a sponsored walk for charity.

   How many pupils did not take part?

2. In a GCSE examination forty-five per cent of a school's entry of two hundred pupils gained a grade C or better.

   How many pupils was this?

3. The attendance rate in a school of twelve hundred pupils improves from ninety-five per cent to ninety-seven per cent in consecutive weeks.

   How many more children were present in the second week?

4. Eight kilometres is about five miles.

   On an activity holiday pupils will cycle between two hostels forty kilometres apart.

   About how many miles is this?

5. Pupils spent twenty-five hours in lessons each week. Four hours a week were allocated to mathematics.

   What percentage of lesson time per week was spent on other subjects?

6. As part of a practical science workshop some teachers will watch a demonstration lesson of 70 minutes which will be followed by a discussion for 30 minutes. If the demonstration started at oh-nine-thirty, what time will the workshop end?

7. A teacher travels from school to a training course. After the course is over she returns to school. The distance to the training venue is twenty-four miles and expenses are paid at a rate of forty pence per mile. How much will she receive?

8. What is 15 per cent as a decimal?

9. In a mock GCSE examination taken by a class of 30 pupils, 25 pupils gained a grade 5 and 2 pupils gained a grade 6. No pupil gained a higher grade. What percentage of pupils gained a grade 4 or below?

10. A test is marked out of 60. Pupils need 75 per cent to achieve grade A. How many marks is this?

11. The school library is open for 5 hours 20 minutes each Monday, Wednesday and Friday, and for 6 hours and 30 minutes each Tuesday and Thursday. What is the total time the library is open during the school week?

12. Two thirds of a class of 27 pupils are judged to be on target for a grade C, or better, result in their GCSE mathematics examination. How many pupils are judged to get a grade D result or worse?

Practice on-screen test

1. In preparation for target setting a teacher at a comprehensive school produced a scatter graph showing comparative GCSE results for 2012 and 2013 for 10 schools, labelled A to J, in the local authority.

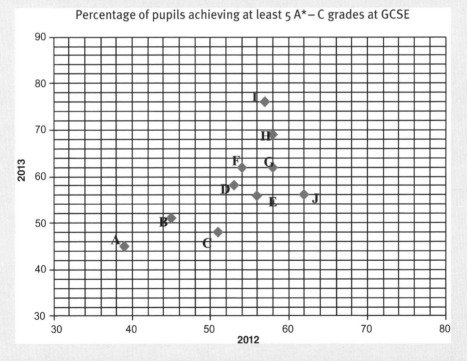

Write down the letters of the two schools whose percentage of pupils achieving at least 5 A*–C grades at GCSE decreased by more than 2% between 2012 and 2013.

(Continued)

(Continued)

2. A careers teacher produced the following pie charts showing the other subjects taken by sixth form students who also chose to study A level mathematics.

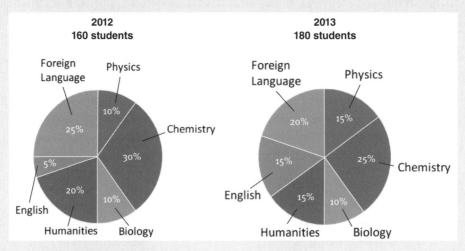

Indicate all the true statements.

A   More pupils chose a foreign language in 2012 than in 2013.

B   More pupils chose chemistry in 2012 than in 2013.

C   10 more pupils chose English in 2012 than in 2013.

3. The table below shows the percentage of students going from a school to different destinations after Year 13.

	2014	2015	2016	2017
Higher education	40	41	43	44
Further education	19	17	19	20
Employment	20	22	21	18
Gap year	14	15	16	17
Other	7	5	1	1

Which destinations showed a continual increase over the four years?

4. A teacher analysed some pupils' results in their mock GCSE examinations in Year 11. She produced the following table showing their predicted grades for English and mathematics.

Subject		Number of pupils achieving each grade			
		Grade D	Grade C	Grade B	Grades A/A*
English	Boys	14	34	32	10
	Girls	13	37	35	15
Mathematics	Boys	28	30	16	9
	Girls	10	45	23	20

Indicate all the true statements.

A   The percentage of boys predicted to gain a grade C in their GCSE mathematics examination is greater than the percentage of boys predicted to gain a grade C in their English examination.

B   A higher percentage of girls than boys are predicted to gain a grade C or grade B in mathematics.

C   The percentage of boys predicted to gain a grade D in mathematics is double the percentage of boys predicted to gain a grade D in English.

5. A teacher worked out the actual age of 3 pupils on the day of a reading test.

The test took place on 23 June 2017, and the ages were calculated to the nearest month.

Pupil	Date of birth	Age
A	21/02/2011	
B	18/07/2011	
C	01/10/2010	

| 6 years 1 month | | 5 years 11 months | | 6 years 4 months | | 6 years 8 months |

What are the correct ages for each pupil?

6. A teacher produced the following chart to show performance of Year 11 pupils in GCSE mathematics in 2013.

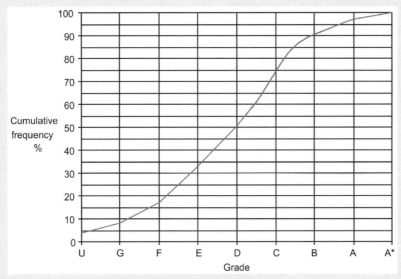

There were 240 pupils in the year group.

What was the number of pupils who achieved a grade B and above in mathematics?

A   10

B   60

C   25

(Continued)

(Continued)

7. The performance in a writing task of pupils in different year groups was determined as part of a research project.

   A teacher produced the following diagram to show the levels children reached in writing in the different year groups.

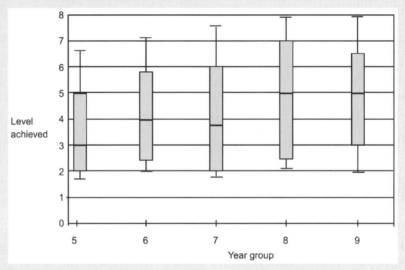

Indicate all the true statements.

A   The median writing level decreased between Year 8 and Year 9.

B   In Year 9, 50% of pupils achieved a writing level of 5 or more.

C   In Year 7, 25% of pupils achieved a writing level of 2 or less.

8. The scatter graph below shows the end of year test results in mathematics and science for a group of Year 7 pupils.

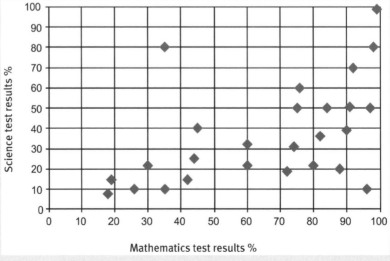

How many pupils achieved more than 60% in at least one of the tests?

9. A head of sixth form uses the following formula to predict A level achievement in points:

$$\text{Predicted A level performance} = \frac{20 \times \text{total GCSE points score}}{\text{number of GCSEs taken}} - 90$$

Student	Total GCSE points score	Number of GCSEs taken	Predicted A level points score, rounded to the nearest whole number
A	28	5	
B	56	8	50
C	45	7	39

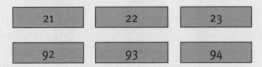

What would be the predicted points score for Student A?

Write (Select and Place) the correct predicted A level performance for Student A in the table.

10. For a trip to Germany pupils have a spending money allowance of £150.

A pupil returns with 30 euros. How much of his allowance did he spend? Give your answer in £.

(use the fact that £1 is equivalent to 1.2 euros).

11. In a GCSE examination the grade boundaries for each of the three higher tier papers are shown below.

Paper	A*	A	B	C	D	E
Paper 1	90	80	70	60	50	45
Paper 2	90	80	70	60	50	45
Paper 3	180	160	140	120	100	90

A pupil's mark for each paper will be added together to give the total final mark.

The following table gives the minimum total mark required for each overall grade.

	A*	A	B	C	D	E
Total uniform mark	360	320	280	240	200	160

A pupil's mark for Paper 1 was 65, his mark for Paper 2 was 75.

What mark does he need to gain on Paper 3 in order to gain a pass at GCSE grade B?

12. A primary school head teacher prepared a chart showing the percentage of pupils who achieved level 4 and above in mathematics in the end of Key Stage 2 tests.

(Continued)

(Continued)

Percentage of pupils achieving level 4 and above in Key Stage 2 mathematics

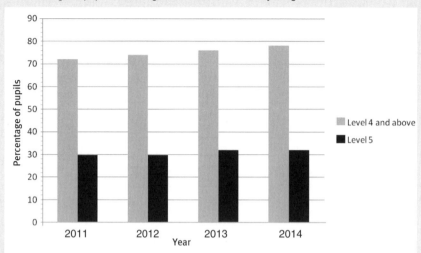

Indicate all the true statements.

A   In each year less than half the pupils achieved below level 5.

B   In 2014, 22% of pupils achieved below level 4.

C   If the trend of achievement continues the percentage of pupils achieving level 4 and above will be 80% in 2016.

13. A history teacher set a coursework exercise for a Year 10 class of 20 students. The students recorded the time at which they completed the exercise. The maximum time allowed was 60 minutes. The pass mark was set at 25 marks out of a possible 45. The teacher prepares a scattergraph to show the relation between the time taken and the mark achieved. Each point represents one student.

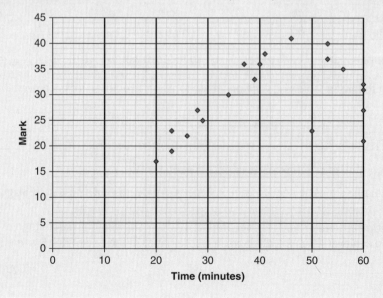

What fraction of students who finished before half the maximum time did not achieve a pass?

A $\dfrac{1}{4}$

B $\dfrac{3}{10}$

C $\dfrac{2}{3}$

14. A teacher prepares a bar chart to compare the percentage of pupils achieving GCSE grades A* to C in mathematics with other GCSE subjects.

    140 pupils sat the GCSE mathematics examination and 90 achieved a GCSE grade A*–C.

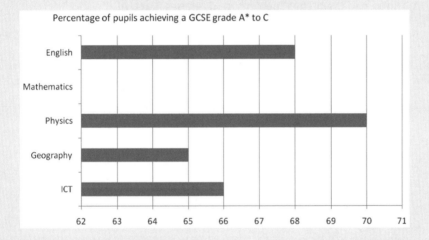

Percentage of pupils achieving a GCSE grade A* to C

Which one of the following bars ought to be placed on the bar chart above to represent the mathematics results?

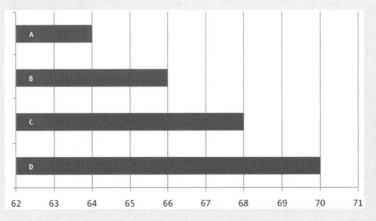

(Continued)

(Continued)

15. This table shows the GCSE grades in design and technology achieved by a school's Year 11 pupils for the period 2011 to 2014.

Grade	A*	A	B	C	D	E	F/G	Total number of students
2011	1	2	2	11	5	6	1	28
2012	6	5	9	13	1	0	0	34
2013	4	7	9	16	4	0	0	40
2014	5	6	8	10	4	2	1	36

Which of the following statements is correct?

A   2012 had the highest percentage of grades A and A*.

B   2011 had the lowest percentage of grade C.

C   Less than 1/4 of pupils gained a grade B in any year.

16. A school report includes grades for each pupil's attainment in each subject.

Grade A is awarded for an average test mark of 72% and above.

Pupil	Mark	Pupil	Mark
A	31	M	7
B	34	N	15
C	12	O	31
D	17	P	23
E	29	Q	26
F	19	R	28
G	24	S	29
H	30	T	33
I	32	U	29
J	28	V	34
K	25	W	30
L	33	X	28

The table above shows the results for an English test for a group of 24 pupils.

If the test was marked out of 36 how many pupils achieved a grade A?

6 | Answers and key points

Chapter 1 Key knowledge

1. (a) $\frac{2}{3}$ (b) $\frac{3}{5}$ (c) $\frac{3}{4}$ (d) $\frac{3}{5}$

> **Key point**
>
> Remember to cancel down until there is no common factor for the numerator and denominator. Also, you ought to know that $\frac{75}{100}$ is $\frac{3}{4}$

2. (a) 0.15 (b) 0.36 (c) 0.65 (d) 0.02

> **Key point**
>
> Remember: to change a percentage into a decimal divide by 100. The rule you may have been given at school, when dividing by 100, is 'move the decimal point 2 places to the left'.

3. (a) 70 (b) 10.35 (c) 162 (d) 22.5

> **Key point**
>
> Do the multiplication, ignoring any decimal points, then insert the decimal point counting from right to left the number of decimal places in the question. Thus $0.6 \times 342 \rightarrow 6 \times 342 = 2052$. There is 1 decimal figure so $0.6 \times 342 = 205.2$

4. (a) 96 (b) 90 (c) 9 (d) 48

> **Key point**
>
> Change each percentage into a decimal.

5. (a) 45   (b) 40   (c) 48   (d) 210

> **Key point**
>
> Either change fractions into decimals and then multiply or multiply by the numerator and then divide by the denominator.

6. (a) 37.5%   (b) 80%   (c) 44%   (d) 80%

> **Key point**
>
> To change into a percentage multiply by 100% and this can be written as $\frac{100}{1}$. Always try to simplify by looking for common factors.
>
> (a) $\frac{3}{8} \times \frac{100}{1} = 3 \times 12.5\% = 37.5\%$ (b) $\frac{4}{5} \times \frac{100}{1} = 4 \times 20\% = 80\%$
>
> (c) $\frac{11}{25} \times \frac{100}{1} = 11 \times 4\% = 44\%$ (d) $\frac{28}{35} \times \frac{100}{1} = \frac{28}{7} \times 20\% = 4 \times 20\% = 80\%$

7. (a) $\frac{17}{20}$ (b) $\frac{3}{10}$ (c) $\frac{16}{25}$ (d) $\frac{3}{50}$

> **Key point**
>
> Cancel down – look for common factors. For example, $85\% = \frac{85}{100}$ and dividing both numbers by 5 gives $\frac{17}{20}$

8. Girls:

    mean = 50 (to the nearest whole number)
    median = 48
    mode = 48
    range = 63 − 45 = 18

For both boys and girls the median, mode and range are the same but the mean for the girls is slightly higher so one could deduce that the girls are slightly better than the boys, but the difference is not significant. (Don't worry – you will not be asked to do an analysis like this!)

Chapter 2 Mental arithmetic

1. 55 minutes

> **Key point**
>
> Count on from 1 hour 20 minutes.

2. 28

Key point

70% of 40 = 0.7 × 40 or $\frac{17}{20}$ × 40

3. 17

Key point

Note: 100 ÷ 6 = 16.666 therefore 17

4. 75%

Key point

The number of pupils is 3 × 28 = 84. The fraction is therefore $\frac{63}{84}$. The common factor is 7 therefore the fraction simplifies to $\frac{9}{12} = \frac{3}{4}$ which is 75%.

5. 9

Key point

Note: 450 ÷ 52 = 8.65, therefore 9

6. 48

Key point

Calculate as 30 ÷ 5 = 6, then 6 × 8 = 48 or 8 ÷ 5 = 1.6 so 30 × 1.6 = 3 × 16 = 48

7. 12:40

Key point

Count on 1 hour 10 minutes + 2 hours.

8. 11

Key point

10 rows for 400 people, so one more row needed for the remaining 32

9. 84%

> **Key point**
>
> 21 hours remaining $= \dfrac{21}{25} = 84\%$

10. 123

> **Key point**
>
> The calculation is: $15 \times 4 + 9 \times 5 + 6 \times 3 = 60 + 45 + 18 = 123$

11. 8%

> **Key point**
>
> Remember: to convert fractions with denominators of 25 to a percentage, multiply the numerator by 4: $\dfrac{22}{25} = 88\%$, therefore 8% difference.

12. £500

> **Key point**
>
> Simplify quickly by changing into £: $200 \times 50 \times 5\text{p} = £2 \times 50 \times 5$

13. 60%

> **Key point**
>
> Common factor is 7, therefore $\dfrac{42}{70} = \dfrac{6}{10} = 60\%$

14. 720p or £7.20

> **Key point**
>
> Work out as $120 \times 2 \times 3 = 120 \times 6$

15. 0.075

Key point

Think of $7\frac{1}{2}$ % as 7.5% then divide by 100.

16. 15

Key point

Work out as $\frac{3}{7} \times 35$

17. 265

Key point

$(5 \times 25) + (5 \times 28)$

18. 22 hours and 5 minutes

Key point

$5 \times (4hr\ 25\ mins) = (5 \times 4hr) + (5 \times 25\ min) = 20hr + 125mins = 20hr + 2hr\ 5\ mins$

19. 68%

Key point

$18 + 16 = 34$ then double

20. 36

Key point

First calculate 80% of 120 which is $0.8 \times 120 = 96$ (so 96 pupils achieved level 4 or level 5). Then subtract the pupils who achieved level 5, that is 60 pupils, leaving 36.

21. 2 days

> **Key point**
>
> 0.4 × 5 days = 2 days

22. 0.625

> **Key point**
>
> The fraction is $\frac{54}{144}$. You now need to simplify this. You might recognise that 18 is a common factor, but if not then divide by 2 giving $\frac{27}{72}$ and then by 9 giving $\frac{3}{8}$. This then is the fraction who travel by bus. Therefore the fraction who don't travel by bus is $\frac{5}{8}$ and you should recognise this as 0.625 Alternatively you could first find the number who don't travel by bus, 144 − 54 = 90. Then express that as a fraction, $\frac{90}{144}$, divide by 18 or divide by 2, then by 3 and by 3 again, and get $\frac{5}{8}$ which is 0.625.

23. 6.25m^2

> **Key point**
>
> The calculation is 2.5 × 2.5. You should know that 25^2 is 625.

24. 12

> **Key point**
>
> Quicker to find 40% or 0.4 × 30 = 12

25. 96

> **Key point**
>
> The calculation is, using the formula: Time = distance ÷ speed, $\frac{40}{25}$ × 60 (the × 60 is to change the answer into minutes) which simplifies to $\frac{8}{5}$ × 60 and then to 8 × 12.

26. 63

> **Key point**
>
> The calculation is 0.2 × 315 = 63.

27. $\dfrac{3}{4}$

> **Key point**
>
> The lesson is 80 minutes long. There are 60 minutes left for the assessment and as a fraction this is $\dfrac{60}{80} = \dfrac{3}{4}$.

28. 3

> **Key point**
>
> $12\dfrac{1}{2}\%$ is $\dfrac{1}{8}$ – you should know this. $\dfrac{1}{8}$ of $24 = 3$

29. 14

> **Key point**
>
> Find $\dfrac{1}{5}$ and double to give $\dfrac{2}{5} \times 35 = 14$

30. 24%

> **Key point**
>
> $\dfrac{6}{25}$ gained less than half marks; multiply the numerator and denominator by 4 to give $\dfrac{24}{100} = 24\%$

31. 0.125

> **Key point**
>
> Write it as 12.5 and divide by 100.

32. 405.6

> **Key point**
>
> Simple to multiply by 100 but be careful!

33. 60%

> **Key point**
>
> Either start with the fraction $\dfrac{2}{5}$ who don't speak English. This is equivalent to 40% so 60% speak English, or work with $\dfrac{3}{5}$ who do speak English and this is 60%.

34. 9:35

Key point

Treat 40 minutes as 30 minutes + 10 minutes, i.e. 8:55 $\longrightarrow$ 9:25 $\longrightarrow$ 9:35

35. 110

Key point

20% + 25% = 45% so 55% play football

36. 6.25km

Key point

The calculation is 25 × 10 × 25 = 6250 metres, then divide by 1000 to change into kilometres giving 6.25.

37. $\frac{2}{3}$

Key point

Either: find the number who do stay in full-time education. This is 144 − 48 = 96. Then express this as a fraction and simplify it: $\frac{96}{144} = \frac{8}{12} = \frac{2}{3}$. Or express those who do not stay in full-time education as a fraction and subtract. Thus $\frac{48}{144} = \frac{1}{3}$ so $\frac{2}{3}$ stay.

38. £19.20

Key point

The calculation is 2 × 24 × 0.4

39. 9

Key point

Either work out the number staying on = 0.7 × 30 = 21 and then subtract from 30 giving 9, or work with the proportion leaving, 0.3 and 0.3 × 30 = 9

40. 500ml

> **Key point**
>
> The calculation is $20 \times 25 = 500$

41. 16

> **Key point**
>
> $31 \div 4 = 7\frac{3}{4}$ so 8 groups needed, $8 \times 2 = 16$

42. £257.60

> **Key point**
>
> Find 10% of £224 = £22.40. Find 5% by halving the 10% answer = £11.20. Add these to get £33.60. £224 + £33.60 = £257.60

43. £150

> **Key point**
>
> The calculation is $15 \times 2.5 \times 4$

44. £100

> **Key point**
>
> Cost of 2 nights = €55 × 2 = €110. Divide by 1.1 gives £100

45. $\frac{1}{6}$

> **Key point**
>
> You need to add $\frac{1}{2}$ and $\frac{1}{3}$. $\frac{1}{2} + \frac{1}{3} = \frac{3}{6} + \frac{2}{6} = \frac{5}{6}$ so $\frac{1}{6}$ study Chinese.

Chapter 3 Solving written arithmetic problems

1. Mean = 29.7; mode = 24; range = 17

Answers and key points

Key point

$$\text{Mean} = \frac{19\times2+24\times8+27\times1+29\times5+33\times2+34\times5+36\times7}{30} = \frac{890}{30} = 29.7$$

Mode = most frequent mark. This is 24 because it occurs the most – 8 times. It is not the number of times it occurs. Range = highest mark (36) – lowest mark (19) = 17.

2. £87.72

Key point

€100 = £$\frac{100}{1.14}$ = £87.719. Remember that money has only 2 decimal places so round up to £87.72

3. 25

Key point

30 pupils scored either 100 or 101. Ratio is 5:1. Divide 30 by (5 + 1) = 5 so 1 part = 5 so 25 pupils scored 100 (and 5 scored 101).

4. School A

Key point

Score of 100 or 101. School A = $\frac{22}{33}$ = 66.7%; School B = $\frac{21}{32}$ = 65.6%; School C = $\frac{23}{35}$ = 65.7%

5. 10 below

Key point

Find 18% of 250 = 0.18 × 250 = 45, so 10 below

6. A, B and C

Key point

You need to calculate the total number of pupils for each year – 2016 has 42, 2015 has 35, 2014 has 48, 2013 has 48.

A   % gaining A or B in 2013 is $\frac{37}{48}$ = 77%. In 2016 is $\frac{34}{42}$ = 81% so true.

B   In 2015, % failing to get A = $\frac{21}{35}$ = 60%. In 2014 it is $\frac{25}{48}$ = 52% so true.

C   % gaining A in 2016 = $\frac{19}{42}$ = 45%. In 2015 it is $\frac{14}{35}$ = 40% so true.

7. 3

Key point

25% of 6 hours is 1 hour 30 minutes so 2 sessions (80 minutes) is too short.

8. A

Key point

The calculation is $\left(\frac{58}{75} \times 0.6\right) + \left(\frac{65}{125} \times 0.4\right) = 0.464 + 0.208 = 0.672$, i.e. 67.2%

9. Test 3

Key point

Convert to percentages.

10. Classes 7SW, 7MP, 7TS

Key point

Multiply the number of pupils in each class by 2/3.

11. A, B

Key point

By inspection you can save time! A mean score of 16 cannot come from pupils B and C – the highest score for B is 15 and for C is 14.

12. (a) 1%   (b) 2013

Key point

(a) in 2014 $\frac{84}{110} = 76\%$ (b) you will have to work out and compare the percentages for the years 2011–14 – you have already worked out the value for 2014.

13. A, B

Key point

Remember that, for example, $-3 < d \leq -6$ means that the difference, d, cannot be -3 but could lie between -3.1 and -6.

(Continued)

Answers and key points

(*Continued*)

A Boys is $1+3+3+2=9$. Girls is $1+1+2=4$
B Girls is $1+3+3+2=9$ so proportion $=\dfrac{9}{15}=0.6$
C We do not know exactly how many are actually 12 months or more above their actual age.

14. School Q

Key point

Change each figure into decimals:

$\dfrac{2}{9}=0.222$ 57 out of $300=0.19$ $18\%=0.18$

15. 11

Key point

Look at the second table. To score a scaled score of less than 100 the marks have to be less than 59.

16. 4.5

Key point

Use a ruler to help – find 6 on the horizontal axis and read off the corresponding value on the vertical axis.

17. 28%

Key point

Because the times both involve half hours, it is simply working out $\dfrac{6.5}{23.5}\times100=27.66\%=28\%$ to the nearest per cent.

18. 50%

Key point

Subtract, remembering 12 months in a year. Pupils A, C, E, G, H fit the criterion.

19. $\dfrac{35}{60}=\dfrac{7}{12}$

Key point

Count pupil numbers carefully – jot down totals.

20. 15

> **Key point**
>
> $1500 \div 100 = 15$

21. A

> **Key point**
>
> Number of 'pupil laps' = $(65 \times 8 + 94 \times 10) = 1460$
>
> Total distance = $1460 \times 700 = 1022\,000$ metres = $1\,022$km

22. 10

> **Key point**
>
> Use a sketch – 3 small sheets per width of large sheet.

23. (a) 35   (b) 39

> **Key point**
>
> (a) Remember to order the percentage marks.
>
> (b) Total = $36 + 47 + 34 + 33 + 45 = 195$ so mean is $195 \div 5 = 39$

24. A

> **Key point**
>
> For A: 2013 has $3/28 = 10.7\%$; 2014 has $11/34 = 32.4\%$; 2015 has $11/40 = 27.5\%$; 2016 has $11/36 = 30.6\%$. Note 2014, 2015 and 2016 all have 11 pupils gaining A or A* so the biggest % is when the denominator of each fraction is smallest – if you spot this you can save some time.
>
> For B: the fractions are: 11/28, 13/34, 16/40, 10/36; 16/40 is a higher % than the others.
>
> For C: finding ¼ of the pupil numbers gives in 2013 → 7, 2 is less than 7, in 2014 → 8.5, but 9 is more than 8.5 so statement C is not true.

25. (a) 192km   (b) 31 miles (actually 31.25)

> **Key point**
>
> The calculations are: (a) $120 \times \dfrac{8}{5}$ (b) $50 \times \dfrac{5}{8}$

26. 0.1mm

> **Key point**
>
> Take care with the units – work in millimetres, i.e. $50 \div 500$.

27. 33%

> **Key point**
>
> The fraction is $\frac{20}{60}$ so as a percentage this is 33.3333%, i.e. 33% to the nearest whole number.

28. 128cm

> **Key point**
>
> You can fit 8 lots of 15cm across the 120cm width.

29. 5:30 a.m.

> **Key point**
>
> Remember time = distance ÷ speed. The travel time = $120 \div 40 = 3$ hours. Add 0.5 hour, therefore total time = 3.5 hours.

30. 16km

> **Key point**
>
> Total map distance = 32.3cm = $32.3 \times 50\,000$cm on the ground = 16.15km

31. 363.6 seconds = 6 minutes 3.6 seconds

> **Key point**
>
> Add up the time in seconds and decimals of seconds giving 363.6 seconds then convert.

32. £65.88; £83.88

> **Key point**
>
> Remember to work in £ on the mileage rate.

33. 28 pupils

> **Key point**
>
> From 9:00 to 10:30 is 90 minutes ⟶ she can see 4 pupils.
> From 10:45 to 12:00 is 75 minutes ⟶ she can see 3 pupils.
> Total for the day = 7 pupils, total over 4 days = 28 pupils.
> If the calculations were done using the total figures:
> her working week = 4 × 3 hours less 4 × 15 minutes = 11 hours
> 11 hours = 660 minutes ÷ 20, giving 33 pupils
> This would be incorrect because it ignores the 'structure' of the school morning.

34. 1.514m

> **Key point**
>
> The total height for the 20 girls = 20 × 1.51 = 30.2m
> The new total height = 30.2 + 1.6 = 31.8 m but this is for 21 girls
> The new mean height = 31.8 ÷ 21 = 1.514m

35. (a) Test 1   (b) 0.3

> **Key point**
>
> (a) The range for test 1 is −10 to 10 which is 20.
>   The range for test 2 is −9 to 10 which is 19.
>   So test 1.
> (b) 5 pupils made no progress so as a fraction this is $\frac{5}{16}$ which equals 0.3125. This rounds to 0.3.

36. 8 layers

> **Key point**
>
> The calculation, working in centimetres, is 124 ÷ 15 = 8.266, so round down.

37. 18

> **Key point**
>
> There are two ways of solving this: The first way would be to (a) find the number studying maths. This is 20% of 150 = 30. (b) Find the number studying chemistry – 8% of 150 = 12, and then find the difference: 30 – 12 = 18.
>
> The second way would be to find the difference in the percentages: 20% – 8% = 12%. Then find 12% of 150 = 18.

38. 11:20

> **Key point**
>
> 400km = 250 miles

39. A

> **Key point**
>
> Raw score of 52 gives from the graph a UMS value of 76. From the table this results in a grade A.

40. 25

> **Key point**
>
> Sample size = 10 + 150 ÷ 10 = 25

41. A, B

> **Key point**
>
> Remember to go down columns for maths and French and along rows for English.
>
> A   Number gaining A^*–C in French is 20 + 40 = 60 out of a total of 80. % = $\dfrac{60}{80}$ = 75%.
>
> B   In the maths table, 38 gained A^*–A in English and 57 gained B–C so 38 + 57 = 95 gained C or above in English. This is more than half of 120.
>
> C   In French, 16 + 3 + 1 = 20 did not achieve a grade C or above. This is $\dfrac{1}{4}$ of 80 so not true.

42. B, E, G, H

43. 72

44. 55

45. B and C are true.

46. 53

47. 30

48. 98

Key point

Total of the scores is $2 + 5 + 4 + 7 = 18$. Read across the table along the row with 18 and the score in the column headed 6.10 is 98.

49. 7.5km/h

Key point

Speed = distance ÷ time = $6 ÷ 0.8$ (NB work in hours, 48 mins = $\frac{4}{5}$hr = 0.8 hr)

50. 23.67

Key point

You must work out $20 ÷ 15$ first, not $25 × 20$ then divide by 15.
Therefore reading level = $5 + (20 - 1.33) = 5 + 18.67 = 23.67$

51. 5.51

Key point

The total points are given by $(4 × 5) + (4 × 6) + (1 × 7) + (1 × 8) = 59$
The calculation is then $(\frac{59}{10}$ x $3.9) - 17.5 = 5.51$

52. 87

Key point

The calculation is $80 = A × 0.6 + 70 × 0.4$
$$80 = A × 0.6 + 28$$
Therefore $A × 0.6 = 52$
$$A = 52 ÷ 0.6 = 86.67, \text{ i.e. } 87$$

53. A

Key point

Remember that the table lists %.

A   35% gained A*–A. 35% of 80 = 28, so true.

B   8% of 25 = 2; 5% of 60 = 3, so not true.

C   80 gained A*–C in English. 42 gained A*–A, so not true.

54. 18

Key point

$\frac{3}{4} - \frac{1}{2} = \frac{1}{4}$ so $\frac{1}{4}$ receive an award.

55. 9.6

Key point

Work out brackets first.

56. B, C

Key point

A   School A had no change in 2014, 2015.

B   Range of values for 2013–16: A is 5 percentage points, B is 24, C is 13 and D is 12.

C   School B is 81%; School D is 69%

57. $\frac{1}{4}$

Key point

Cost = £280 + 35 × £8 = £560. Pupils pay 35 × £12 = £420. School pays £560 – £420 = £140.
Fraction is $\frac{140}{560} = \frac{1}{4}$

58. 57.1

Key point

Total for 26 pupils = 26 × 56 = 1456. New total = 1456 + 86 = 1542
New mean = 1542 ÷ 27

59. 15

Key point

75% of 36 = 27. So count pupils with a mark of 27 or more.

60. (a) £132   (b) £24

Key point

(a) The cost of separate tickets for 1 student is £4.50 + £3.50 = £8.00. So for 66 students the cost = 66 × £8.00 = £528. The cost of 66 combined tickets is 66 × £6 = £396. The saving is £528 – £396 = £132.

(b) 66 students will require 4 adults (note: 3 adults will only 'cover' 60 students). 2 adults will be free – since 66 is greater than 60. So only 2 adults will have to pay. Cost = 2 × £12.00 = £24.00.

61. £38

Key point

The calculation can be broken down into stages:

- the number of gallons used $= \dfrac{200}{32} = 6.25$;
- the number of litres $= 6.25 \times 4.546 = 28.4125$;
- the cost $= 28.4125 \times £1.34 = £38.07$ which rounds to £38.

When you do these sorts of calculations try to avoid rounding any intermediate answers and round when you get the final answer.

62. (a) Science   (b) 0.15

Key point

(a) % pupils achieving grades 6 or 7:

English: number of boys $= 48+32 = 80$. $\% = \dfrac{80}{120} = 66.7\%$

Number of girls $= 48+40 = 88$. $\% = \dfrac{88}{112} = 78.6\%$

Maths: number of boys $= 56+32 = 88$. $\% = \dfrac{88}{120} = 73.3\%$

$$\text{Number of girls} = 52+32 = 84. \% = \frac{84}{112} = 75\%$$

$$\text{Science: number of boys} = 56+36 = 92. \% = \frac{92}{120} = 76.7\%$$

$$\text{Number of girls} = 52+32 = 84. \% = \frac{84}{112} = 75\%$$

Thus in science the percentage of boys achieving level 6 and above was greater than the percentage of girls.

(b) Total number of boys achieving levels 5, 6 and 7 = 20 + 48 + 32 = 100

Therefore 120 −100 = 20 did not.

Total number of girls achieving levels 5, 6, and 7 = 10 + 48 + 40 = 98

Therefore 112 − 98 = 14 did not.

Total who did not achieve levels 5, 6 and 7 = 20 + 14 = 34

Total pupils = 120 + 112 = 232

$$\frac{34}{232} = 0.14655 \text{ so } 0.15$$

Chapter 4 Interpreting and using written data

1. (a) 6   (b) No   (c) Yes

Key point

(a) Find 2 on the Key Stage 2 axis and move up the graph until you reach the median line. Read off the value on the GCSE axis.

(b) Find 11 on the GCSE axis and 5 on the Key Stage 2 axis. The lines through these values intersect in the space between the lower quartile line and the median line so it is not true – remember that 25% of the pupils are below the lower quartile.

(c) Find 4 on the Key Stage 2 axis, 50% lie between 8 (the lower quartile) and 12 (the upper quartile).

2. A, C

Key point

For answer B note that 21 out of 28 is 75%. For 75% of the pupils to achieve over 40% of the marks the whole box and the upper whisker must start at or be above a mark of 40%. This is only true for classes 10C and 10D.

3. A and B are true.

> ## Key point
>
> A. Oral range = 80 − 25 = 55; written range = 70 − 25 = 45.
>
> B. Imagine a line drawn from (0, 0) to (100, 100). This is the line where scores on both tests were the same. There are 4 points above this line, $\dfrac{4}{16} = \dfrac{1}{4}$
>
> C. Lowest written marks are 25 and 35, both pupils scoring 30 in the oral, but another pupil scored 25 in the oral.

4. B and C are true.

> ## Key point
>
> A. This is false. The upper quartile is at 73, so 1/4 of all the pupils scored more than 73 marks, not 70.
>
> B. Median is at 60 so true.
>
> C. Range = 90 − 25 = 65 so true.

5. B is true.

> ## Key point
>
> It is important to realise that, although the pie charts appear to be the same size, they represent different 'quantities' – 800 children and 1000 children.
>
> Statement A is not true. 50% of 800 = 40% of 1000
>
> $\qquad$ (0.5 × 800 = 400 and 0.4 × 1000 = 400)
>
> Statement B is true. 20% of 1000 is more than 20% of 800
>
> $\qquad$ (0.2 × 1000 = 200, 0.2 × 800 = 160)
>
> Statement C is not true. 10% of 800 = 80

6. (a) Test 3 $\qquad$ (b) Only A is true.

> ## Key point
>
> Remember that each 'part' of a box and whisker plot represents 25%.

7. Only C is true.

> ## Key point
>
> 140 pupils get D and below, 170 get C and below so 30 get grade C.

8. (a) 170   (b) £15

> **Key point**
>
> (a) Add up the values given by the tops of each bar:
>
>   22 + 20 + 15 + 20 + 9 + 25 + 20 + 20 + 15 + 4
>
> (b) The modal amount is that received by the most children, i.e. £15 received by 25 children.

9. B and C are true.

> **Key point**
>
> A is not true. Pupils V, X and Y have 2 years with the same mark.
>
> B is true – while it is unlikely, the indications are that pupil Z's marks go up by 2 each test.
>
> C is true – the mean is 18 – add the marks (=90) divide by 5. The median is 18 – the middle value when the marks are put in order – and the mode is 18.

10. A and B are true.

> **Key point**
>
> A. Medians are 102 and 93.
> B. Interquartile range for B = 106 − 88.
> C. School A range = 119 − 70, school B range = 120 − 78.

11. A and B are true.

> **Key point**
>
> A. 50% lie above the median line which is at 93.
> B. 25% lie below the lower quartile which is from 88 and below.
> C. IQ range for A = 24 and for B = 18.

12. A and B are true.

> **Key point**
>
> A. 6 pupils on the line of equal scores – so true.
> B. True – gained 85 and is the greatest distance above the line.
> C. Not true – 7 pupils below the line.

13. (a) 1.6   (b) 1.5

> ### *Key point*
>
> (a) Simple subtraction   (b) Simple calculation of the mean

14. A and C are true.

> ### *Key point*
>
> A. History 'box' extends from F to C.
> B. History has a lower median grade.
> C. German median is at grade C so 50% gained C to A*.

15. About 45–49 marks

> ### *Key point*
>
> You need to draw in the line of best fit through the points.

16. A and B are true.

> ### *Key point*
>
> A. D lies on the line.
> B. C is to the right of but below B.
> C. A is above the line so A also achieved better than might have been predicted.

17. Z

18. C and D are true.

> ### *Key point*
>
> A. Range for A = 85 − 45 = 40, range for B = 90 − 40 = 50
> B. Lowest value for A = 45 and for B = 40
> C. Imagine a line drawn from (0, 0) to (100, 100), 8 pupils on or below the line and $\frac{8}{20} = 40\%$
> D. 14 scored over 60% in Test A and 13 scored over 60% in Test B

19. B and C are true.

> ### Key point
>
> A. Pupil F score decreased.
> B. Pupil B score increased by 11.
> C. Two pupils (D, F) had lower scores.

20. A, B, C

21. Schools B and D

> ### Key point
>
> B and D are the only two schools with values increasing each year.

22. A and C are true.

> ### Key point
>
> A. is true – level 7 in science for single-sex classes and 6 for the mixed classes.
> B. is not true – the level achieved for the girls only classes was the same as the mixed classes.
> C. is true – the girls only classes achieved level 8 compared with level 7 for the mixed classes.

23. A, C

> ### Key point
>
> A True – in 2013–14 61.2% – 59.0% = 2.2%
> B Not true. English decreased in 2015.
> C English is 76.5% – 75.8% = 0.7%; Maths is 71.4% – 69.6% = 1.8%; Science is 64% – 59% = 5%.

24. B and C are true.

> ### Key point
>
> A. is not true – the lowest mark is for class 7A at about 6.
> B. is true – the median mark in class 7C is 50, in class 7A it is 40.
> C. is true – the 'upper' whisker starts at 70.

Chapter 5 Practice mental arithmetic test answers

Note that units will not have to be entered in the test – the appropriate unit should appear in the answer box.

1. 60

2. 90

3. 24

4. 25 (miles)

5. 84 (%)

6. 11:10

7. (£) 19.20

8. 0.15

9. 10 (%)

10. 45 (marks)

11. 29 (hours)

12. 9

Practice on-screen test answers

1. C and J

> **Key point**
>
> In an actual test this question could be worded as follows: 'Point and click on the letters of the two schools ...' You may find it useful to imagine the line where the percentages are equal for each year, i.e. the line joining (30, 30) and (80, 80). On the screen you could use the edge of a piece of paper for the straight line.

2. A, B

> **Key point**
>
> Note that the pie charts represent different totals.
>
> A. is true – 25% of 160 = 40, 20% of 180 = 36
>
> B. is true – 30% of 160 = 48, 25% of 180 = 45
>
> C. is not true – 5% of 160 = 8, 15% of 180 = 27

3. Higher education and gap year

Key point

Remember you are looking for continual improvement.

4. Only B is true.

Key point

This question refers to percentages. The table gives actual numbers. You will have to calculate the totals for each row.

5. A is 6 years 4 months   B is 5 years 11 months   C is 6 years 8 months

Key point

Remember to round the number of months up, or down, to the nearest month.

6. B

Key point

75% gained a grade C or below so 25% gained a grade B, A, A*. 25% of 240 = 60

7. B and C are true.

Key point

Look at the notes about box plots if you are unsure how to interpret them.

8. 16

Key point

Imagine a vertical line drawn through the 60% maths result – how many pupils are to the right of this? Imagine a line drawn through the 60% science result. How many pupils are above this line? Be sure, however, not to count pupils twice.

Answers and key points

9. 22

> **Key point**
>
> Using the simple on-screen calculator you will need to work out the numerator and jot the answer down, then do the division (here divide by 5) and then subtract 90.

10. £125

> **Key point**
>
> 30 euros = £30 ÷ 1.2 = £25. £150 − £25 = £125

11. 140

> **Key point**
>
> Paper 1 mark was 65, Paper 2 mark was 75. Total = 140. For a grade B pass his total mark must be 280 so he needs to score 140 on Paper 3.

12. Only B is true.

> **Key point**
>
> The trend of achievement suggests that the level 4 figures increase by 2 each year and this would indicate that the 80% figure would be reached in 2015 not 2016.

13. C

> **Key point**
>
> There were six students who finished at 30 minutes or less. Four of these did not pass.

14. A

> **Key point**
>
> 90 ÷ 140 = 64.28% so bar A is the best choice.

15. Only A is correct.

> **Key point**
>
> Note that the table quotes actual numbers not percentages so you will need to work these out. For example, in 2012, 11 pupils gained grades A and A*. 11 out of 34 = 32%

16. 16

> **Key point**
>
> First find 72% of 36. This is 25.92, i.e. 26 marks. Next count all those whose mark was 26 or more.

Further reading

You can get further help and guidance with mathematical knowledge from other Learning Matters publications such as:

Mooney, C., Hansen, A., Ferrie, L., Fox, S., and Wrathmell, R. (2018) *Primary Mathematics: Knowledge and Understanding* (8th edition). Exeter: Learning Matters.

Details of publications can be found online at *www.uk.sagepub.co.uk/learningmatters*

Glossary

Accuracy The degree of precision given in the question or required in the answer. For example, a length might be measured to the nearest centimetre. A pupil's reading age is usually given to the nearest month, whilst an average (mean) test result might be rounded to one decimal place.

Bar chart A chart where the number associated with each item is shown either as a horizontal or a vertical bar and where the length of the bar is proportional to the number it represents. The length of the bar is used to show the number of times the item occurs, or the value of the item being measured.

Bar chart showing number of pupils achieving each level

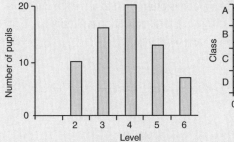

Bar chart arranged horizontally showing mean test scores for four classes

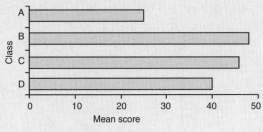

Box and whisker diagram Diagram showing the range and quartile values for a set of data.

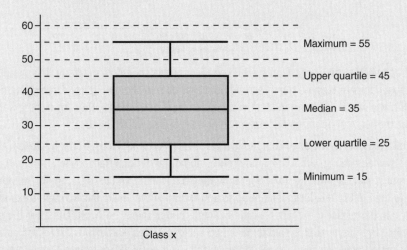

Cohort A group having a common quality or characteristic. For example, 'pupils studying GCSE German this year have achieved higher grades than last year's cohort' (pupils studying GCSE German last year).

Consistent Following the same pattern or style over time with little change. For example, a pupil achieved marks of 84%, 82%, 88% and 85% in a series of mock GCSE tests; her performance was judged to be consistently at the level needed to obtain GCSE grade A*.

Conversion The process of exchanging one set of units for another. Measurement and currency, for example, can be converted from one unit to another, e.g. centimetres to metres, pounds to euros. Conversion of one unit to the other is usually done by using a rule (e.g. 'multiply by $\frac{5}{8}$ to change kilometres into miles'), a formula (e.g. $F = \frac{9}{5}C + 32$, for converting degrees Celsius to degrees Fahrenheit), or a conversion graph.

Correlation The extent to which two quantities are related. For example, there is a positive correlation between two tests, A and B, if a person with a high mark in test A is likely to have a high mark in test B and a person with a low mark in test A is likely to get a low mark in test B. A scatter graph of the two variables may help when considering whether a correlation exists between the two variables.

Cumulative frequency graph A graph in which the frequency of an event is added to the frequency of those that have preceded it. This type of graph is often used to answer a question such as, 'How many pupils are under nine years of age in a local education authority (LA)?' or 'What percentage of pupils gained at least the pass mark of 65 on a test?'.

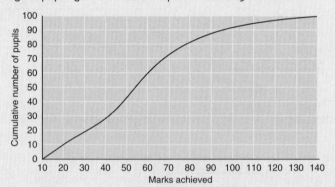

The graph shows the marks pupils achieved. Two pupils scored 10 marks or less, 30 pupils scored 42 marks or less, 60 pupils scored 60 marks or less and 90 pupils scored 95 marks or less. If these were results from a test with a pass mark of 65 marks, then from the graph we can see that 63% of pupils gained 64 marks or less, and so failed the test.

Decimal Numbers based on or counted in a place value system of tens. Normally we talk about decimals when dealing with tenths, hundredths and other decimal fractions less than 1. A decimal point is placed after the units digit in writing a decimal number, eg. 1.25 The number of digits to the right of the decimal point up to and including the final non-zero digit is expressed as the number of decimal places. In the example above there are two digits after the decimal point, and the number is said to have two decimal places, sometimes expressed as 2 dp. Many simple fractions cannot be expressed exactly as a decimal. For example, the fraction $\frac{1}{3}$ as a decimal is 0.3333... which is usually represented as 0.3 recurring. Decimals are usually rounded to a specified degree of accuracy, eg. 0.6778 is 0.68 when rounded to 2 dp. 0.5 is always rounded up, so 0.5 to the nearest whole number is 1.

Distribution The spread of a set of statistical information. For example, the number of absentees on a given day in a school is distributed as follows: Monday – 5, Tuesday – 17, Wednesday – 23, Thursday – 12 and Friday – 3. A distribution can also be displayed graphically.

Formula A relationship between numbers or quantities expressed using a rule or an equation. For example, final mark = (0.6 x mark 1) + (0.4 x mark 2).

Fraction Fractions are used to express parts of a whole, e.g. $\frac{3}{4}$. The number below the division line, the denominator, records the number of equal parts into which the number above the division line, the numerator, has been divided.

Frequency The number of times an event or quantity occurs.

Greater than A comparison between two quantities. The symbol > is used to represent 'greater than', eg. 7>2, or >5%.

Interquartile range The numerical difference between the upper quartile and the lower quartile. The lower quartile of a set of data has one quarter of the data below it and three-quarters above it. The upper quartile has three quarters of the data below it and one quarter above it. The inter-quartile range represents the middle 50% of the data.

Line graphs A graph on which the plotted points are joined by a line. It is a visual representation of two sets of related data. The line may be straight or curved. It is often used to show a trend, such as how a particular value is changing over time.

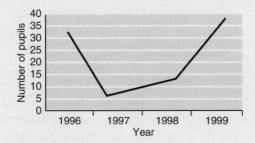

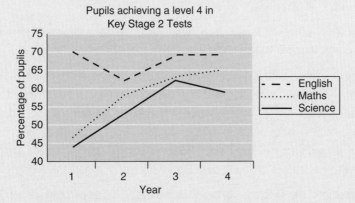

Pupils achieving a level 4 in
Key Stage 2 Tests

Mean One measure of the 'average' of a set of data. The 'mean' average is usually used when the data involved is fairly evenly spread. For example, the individual costs of four textbooks are £9.95, £8.34, £11.65 and £10.50. The mean cost of a textbook is found by totalling the four amounts, giving £40.44, and then dividing by 4, which gives £10.11. The word average is frequently used in place of the mean, but this can be confusing as both median and mode are also ways of expressing an average.

Median Another measure of the 'average' of a set of data. It is the middle number of a series of numbers or quantities when arranged in order, e.g. from smallest to largest. For example, in the following series of number: 2, 4, 5, 7, 8, 15 and 18, the median is 7. When there is an even number of numbers, the median is found by adding the two middle numbers and then halving the total. For example, in the following series of numbers, 12, 15, 23, 30, 31 and 45, the median is $(23 + 30) \div 2 = 26.5$.

Median and quartile lines Quartiles can be found by taking a set of data that has been arranged in increasing order and dividing it into four equal parts. The first quartile is the value of the data at the end of the first quarter. The median quartile is the value of the data at the end of the second quarter. The third quartile is the value of the data at the end of the third quarter.

Quartile lines can be used to show pupils' progression from one key stage to another, when compared with national or local data:

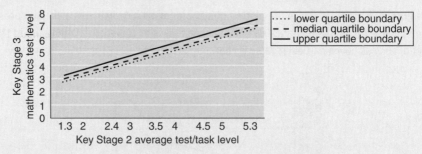

Mode Another measure of the 'average' of a set of data. It is the most frequently occurring result in any group of data. For example, in the following set of exam results: 30%, 34%, 36% 31%, 31%, 30%, 34%, 33%, 31% and 32%, the mode is 31% because this value appears most frequently in the set of results.

Operations The means of combining two numbers or sets of numbers. For example, addition, subtraction, multiplication and division.

Percentage A fraction with a denominator of 100, but written as the numerator followed by '%', e.g. $\frac{30}{100}$ or 30%. A fraction that is not in hundredths can be converted so that the denominator is 100, e.g. $\frac{650}{1000} = \frac{65}{100} = 65\%$. Percentages can be used to compare different fractional quantities. For example, in class A, 10 pupils out of 25 are studying French; in class B, 12 out of 30 pupils are studying French. However, both $\frac{10}{25}$ and $\frac{12}{30}$ are equivalent to $\frac{4}{10}$, or 40%. The same percentage of pupils, therefore, study French in both these classes.

Percentage points The difference between two values, given as percentages. For example, a school has 80% attendance one year and 83% the next year. There has been an increase of 3 percentage points in attendance.

Percentile The values of a set of data that has been arranged in order and divided into 100 equal parts. For example, a year group took a test and the 60th percentile was at a mark of 71. This means that 60% of the cohort scored 71 marks or less. The 25th percentile is the value of the data such that 25% or one quarter of the data is below it and so is the same as the lower quartile. Similarly, the 75th percentile is the same as the upper quartile and the median is the same as the 50th percentile.

Pie chart A pie chart represents the 360° of a circle and is divided into sectors by straight lines from its centre to its circumference. Each sector angle represents a specific proportion of the whole. Pie charts are used to display the relationship of each type or class of data within a whole set of data in a visual form.

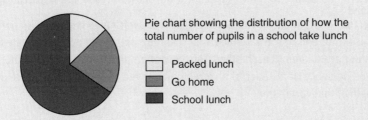

Pie chart showing the distribution of how the total number of pupils in a school take lunch

☐ Packed lunch
▨ Go home
■ School lunch

Prediction A statement based on analysing statistical information about the likelihood that a particular event will occur. For example, an analysis of a school's examination results shows that the number of pupils achieving A*–C grades in science at a school has increased by 3% per year over the past three years. On the basis of this information the school predicts that the percentage of pupils achieving A*–C grades in science at the school next year will increase by at least 2%.

Proportion A relationship between two values or measures. These two values or measures represent the relationship between some part of a whole and the whole itself. For example, a year group of 100 pupils contains 60 boys and 40 girls, so the proportion of boys in the school is 60 out of 100 or 3 out of 5. This is usually expressed as a fraction, in this case, $\frac{3}{5}$.

Quartile (lower) The value of a set of data at the first quarter, 25%, when all the data has been arranged in ascending order. It is the median value of the lower half of all the values in the data set. For example, the results of a test were: 1, 3, 5, 6, 7, 9, 11, 15, 18, 21, 23 and 25. The median is 10. The values in the lower half are 1, 3, 5, 6, 7 and 9. The lower quartile is 5.5. This means that one quarter of the cohort scored 5.5 or less. The lower quartile is also the 25th percentile.

Quartile (upper) The value of a set of data at the third quarter, 75%, when that data has been arranged in ascending order. It is the median value of the upper half of all the values in the data set. In the lower quartile example, the upper quartile is 19.5, the median value of the upper half of the data set. Three quarters of the marks lie below it. The upper quartile is also the 75th percentile.

Range The difference between the lowest and the highest values in a set of data. For example, for the set of data 12, 15, 23, 30, 31 and 45, the range is the difference between 12 and 45. 12 is subtracted from 45 to give a range of 33.

Ratio A comparison between two numbers or quantities. A ratio is usually expressed in whole numbers. For example, a class consists of 12 boys and 14 girls. The ratio of boys to girls is 12:14. This ratio may be described more simply as 6:7 by dividing both numbers by 2. The ratio of girls to boys is 14:12 or 7:6.

Rounding Expressing a number to a degree of accuracy. This is often done in contexts where absolute accuracy is not required, or not possible. For example, it may be acceptable in a report to give outcomes to the nearest hundred or ten. So the number 674 could be rounded up to 700 to the nearest hundred, or down to 670 to the nearest ten. If a number is half way or more between rounding points, it is conventional to round it up, e.g. 55 is rounded up to 60 to the nearest ten and 3.7 is rounded up to 4 to the nearest whole number. If the number is less than half way, it is conventional to round down, eg. 16.43 is rounded down to 16.4 to one decimal place.

Scatter graph A graph on which data relating to two variables is plotted as points, each axis representing one of the variables. The resulting pattern of points indicates how the two variables are related to each other. This type of graph is often used to demonstrate or confirm the presence or absence of a correlation between the two variables, and to judge the strength of that correlation.

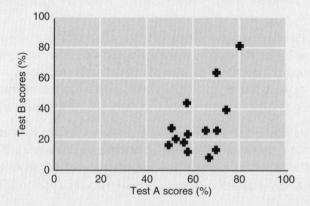

Sector The part or area of a circle which is formed between two radii and the circumference. Each piece of a pie chart is a sector.

Standardised scores Standardised scores are used to enable comparisons on tests between different groups of pupils. Tests are standardised so that the average national standardised scores automatically appear as 100, so it is easy to see whether a pupil is above or below the national average.

Trend The tendency of data to follow a pattern or direction. For example, the trend of the sequence of numbers 4, 7, 11, 13 and 16 is described as 'increasing'.

Value added The relationship between a pupil's previous attainment and their current attainment gives a measure of their progress. Comparing this with the progress made by other pupils gives an impression of the value added by a school. Below is a scatter graph showing progress made by a group of pupils between the end of Key Stage 1 and the end of Key Stage 2:

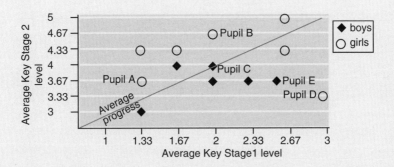

The 'trend line' shows the average performance. Pupils above the line, such as A and B, made better progress than expected; those below the line, such as pupils E and D made less progress than that expected.

How Key Stage 2 relates to Key Stage 1: Median, upper and lower quartile

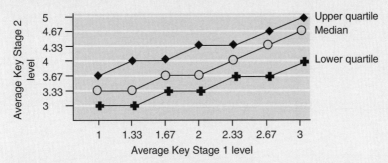

Here the median line shows the national average progress.

Variables The name given to a quantity which can take any one of a given set of values. For example, on a line graph showing distance against time, both distance and time are variables. A variable can also be a symbol which stands for an unknown number, and that can take on different values. For example, the final mark in a test is obtained by a formula using the variables A and B as follows: final mark = (Topic 1 mark x A) + (Topic 2 mark x B).

Weighting A means of attributing relative importance to one or more of a set of results. Each item of data is multiplied by a pre-determined amount to give extra weight to one or more components. For example, marks gained in year 3 of a course may be weighted twice as heavily as those gained in the first two years, in which case those marks would be multiplied by two before finding the total mark for the course.

Whole number A positive integer, eg. 1, 2, 3, 4, 5.

© Teaching Agency